FREE Test Taking Tips DVD Offer

To help us better serve you, we have developed a Test Taking Tips DVD that we would like to give you for FREE. **This DVD covers world-class test taking tips that you can use to be even more successful when you are taking your test.**

All that we ask is that you email us your feedback about your study guide. Please let us know what you thought about it – whether that is good, bad or indifferent.

To get your **FREE Test Taking Tips DVD**, email freedvd@studyguideteam.com with "FREE DVD" in the subject line and the following information in the body of the email:

    a. The title of your study guide.

    b. Your product rating on a scale of 1-5, with 5 being the highest rating.

    c. Your feedback about the study guide. What did you think of it?

    d. Your full name and shipping address to send your free DVD.

If you have any questions or concerns, please don't hesitate to contact us at freedvd@studyguideteam.com.

Thanks again!

GRE Verbal Workbook
GRE Verbal Reasoning Prep with
Three Complete Practice Tests
[3rd Edition Book]

TPB Publishing

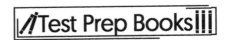

Written and edited by TPB Publishing.

TPB Publishing is not associated with or endorsed by any official testing organization. TPB Publishing is a publisher of unofficial educational products. All test and organization names are trademarks of their respective owners. Content in this book is included for utilitarian purposes only and does not constitute an endorsement by TPB Publishing of any particular point of view.

Interested in buying more than 10 copies of our product? Contact us about bulk discounts:
bulkorders@studyguideteam.com

ISBN 13: 9781628452945
ISBN 10: 1628452943

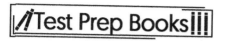

Table of Contents

Quick Overview

As you draw closer to taking your exam, effective preparation becomes more and more important. Thankfully, you have this study guide to help you get ready. Use this guide to help keep your studying on track and refer to it often.

This study guide contains several key sections that will help you be successful on your exam. The guide contains tips for what you should do the night before and the day of the test. Also included are test-taking tips. Knowing the right information is not always enough. Many well-prepared test takers struggle with exams. These tips will help equip you to accurately read, assess, and answer test questions.

A large part of the guide is devoted to showing you what content to expect on the exam and to helping you better understand that content. In this guide are practice test questions so that you can see how well you have grasped the content. Then, answer explanations are provided so that you can understand why you missed certain questions.

Don't try to cram the night before you take your exam. This is not a wise strategy for a few reasons. First, your retention of the information will be low. Your time would be better used by reviewing information you already know rather than trying to learn a lot of new information. Second, you will likely become stressed as you try to gain a large amount of knowledge in a short amount of time. Third, you will be depriving yourself of sleep. So be sure to go to bed at a reasonable time the night before. Being well-rested helps you focus and remain calm.

Be sure to eat a substantial breakfast the morning of the exam. If you are taking the exam in the afternoon, be sure to have a good lunch as well. Being hungry is distracting and can make it difficult to focus. You have hopefully spent lots of time preparing for the exam. Don't let an empty stomach get in the way of success!

When travelling to the testing center, leave earlier than needed. That way, you have a buffer in case you experience any delays. This will help you remain calm and will keep you from missing your appointment time at the testing center.

Be sure to pace yourself during the exam. Don't try to rush through the exam. There is no need to risk performing poorly on the exam just so you can leave the testing center early. Allow yourself to use all of the allotted time if needed.

Remain positive while taking the exam even if you feel like you are performing poorly. Thinking about the content you should have mastered will not help you perform better on the exam.

Once the exam is complete, take some time to relax. Even if you feel that you need to take the exam again, you will be well served by some down time before you begin studying again. It's often easier to convince yourself to study if you know that it will come with a reward!

Test-Taking Strategies

1. Predicting the Answer

When you feel confident in your preparation for a multiple-choice test, try predicting the answer before reading the answer choices. This is especially useful on questions that test objective factual knowledge. By predicting the answer before reading the available choices, you eliminate the possibility that you will be distracted or led astray by an incorrect answer choice. You will feel more confident in your selection if you read the question, predict the answer, and then find your prediction among the answer choices. After using this strategy, be sure to still read all of the answer choices carefully and completely. If you feel unprepared, you should not attempt to predict the answers. This would be a waste of time and an opportunity for your mind to wander in the wrong direction.

2. Reading the Whole Question

Too often, test takers scan a multiple-choice question, recognize a few familiar words, and immediately jump to the answer choices. Test authors are aware of this common impatience, and they will sometimes prey upon it. For instance, a test author might subtly turn the question into a negative, or he or she might redirect the focus of the question right at the end. The only way to avoid falling into these traps is to read the entirety of the question carefully before reading the answer choices.

3. Looking for Wrong Answers

Long and complicated multiple-choice questions can be intimidating. One way to simplify a difficult multiple-choice question is to eliminate all of the answer choices that are clearly wrong. In most sets of answers, there will be at least one selection that can be dismissed right away. If the test is administered on paper, the test taker could draw a line through it to indicate that it may be ignored; otherwise, the test taker will have to perform this operation mentally or on scratch paper. In either case, once the obviously incorrect answers have been eliminated, the remaining choices may be considered. Sometimes identifying the clearly wrong answers will give the test taker some information about the correct answer. For instance, if one of the remaining answer choices is a direct opposite of one of the eliminated answer choices, it may well be the correct answer. The opposite of obviously wrong is obviously right! Of course, this is not always the case. Some answers are obviously incorrect simply because they are irrelevant to the question being asked. Still, identifying and eliminating some incorrect answer choices is a good way to simplify a multiple-choice question.

4. Don't Overanalyze

Anxious test takers often overanalyze questions. When you are nervous, your brain will often run wild, causing you to make associations and discover clues that don't actually exist. If you feel that this may be a problem for you, do whatever you can to slow down during the test. Try taking a deep breath or counting to ten. As you read and consider the question, restrict yourself to the particular words used by the author. Avoid thought tangents about what the author *really* meant, or what he or she was *trying* to say. The only things that matter on a multiple-choice test are the words that are actually in the question. You must avoid reading too much into a multiple-choice question, or supposing that the writer meant something other than what he or she wrote.

5. No Need for Panic

It is wise to learn as many strategies as possible before taking a multiple-choice test, but it is likely that you will come across a few questions for which you simply don't know the answer. In this situation, avoid panicking. Because most multiple-choice tests include dozens of questions, the relative value of a single wrong answer is small. As much as possible, you should compartmentalize each question on a multiple-choice test. In other words, you should not allow your feelings about one question to affect your success on the others. When you find a question that you either don't understand or don't know how to answer, just take a deep breath and do your best. Read the entire question slowly and carefully. Try rephrasing the question a couple of different ways. Then, read all of the answer choices carefully. After eliminating obviously wrong answers, make a selection and move on to the next question.

6. Confusing Answer Choices

When working on a difficult multiple-choice question, there may be a tendency to focus on the answer choices that are the easiest to understand. Many people, whether consciously or not, gravitate to the answer choices that require the least concentration, knowledge, and memory. This is a mistake. When you come across an answer choice that is confusing, you should give it extra attention. A question might be confusing because you do not know the subject matter to which it refers. If this is the case, don't eliminate the answer before you have affirmatively settled on another. When you come across an answer choice of this type, set it aside as you look at the remaining choices. If you can confidently assert that one of the other choices is correct, you can leave the confusing answer aside. Otherwise, you will need to take a moment to try to better understand the confusing answer choice. Rephrasing is one way to tease out the sense of a confusing answer choice.

7. Your First Instinct

Many people struggle with multiple-choice tests because they overthink the questions. If you have studied sufficiently for the test, you should be prepared to trust your first instinct once you have carefully and completely read the question and all of the answer choices. There is a great deal of research suggesting that the mind can come to the correct conclusion very quickly once it has obtained all of the relevant information. At times, it may seem to you as if your intuition is working faster even than your reasoning mind. This may in fact be true. The knowledge you obtain while studying may be retrieved from your subconscious before you have a chance to work out the associations that support it. Verify your instinct by working out the reasons that it should be trusted.

8. Key Words

Many test takers struggle with multiple-choice questions because they have poor reading comprehension skills. Quickly reading and understanding a multiple-choice question requires a mixture of skill and experience. To help with this, try jotting down a few key words and phrases on a piece of scrap paper. Doing this concentrates the process of reading and forces the mind to weigh the relative importance of the question's parts. In selecting words and phrases to write down, the test taker thinks about the question more deeply and carefully. This is especially true for multiple-choice questions that are preceded by a long prompt.

9. Subtle Negatives

One of the oldest tricks in the multiple-choice test writer's book is to subtly reverse the meaning of a question with a word like *not* or *except*. If you are not paying attention to each word in the question, you can easily be led astray by this trick. For instance, a common question format is, "Which of the following is...?" Obviously, if the question instead is, "Which of the following is not...?," then the answer will be quite different. Even worse, the test makers are aware of the potential for this mistake and will include one answer choice that would be correct if the question were not negated or reversed. A test taker who misses the reversal will find what he or she believes to be a correct answer and will be so confident that he or she will fail to reread the question and discover the original error. The only way to avoid this is to practice a wide variety of multiple-choice questions and to pay close attention to each and every word.

10. Reading Every Answer Choice

It may seem obvious, but you should always read every one of the answer choices! Too many test takers fall into the habit of scanning the question and assuming that they understand the question because they recognize a few key words. From there, they pick the first answer choice that answers the question they believe they have read. Test takers who read all of the answer choices might discover that one of the latter answer choices is actually *more* correct. Moreover, reading all of the answer choices can remind you of facts related to the question that can help you arrive at the correct answer. Sometimes, a misstatement or incorrect detail in one of the latter answer choices will trigger your memory of the subject and will enable you to find the right answer. Failing to read all of the answer choices is like not reading all of the items on a restaurant menu: you might miss out on the perfect choice.

11. Spot the Hedges

One of the keys to success on multiple-choice tests is paying close attention to every word. This is never truer than with words like almost, most, some, and sometimes. These words are called "hedges" because they indicate that a statement is not totally true or not true in every place and time. An absolute statement will contain no hedges, but in many subjects, the answers are not always straightforward or absolute. There are always exceptions to the rules in these subjects. For this reason, you should favor those multiple-choice questions that contain hedging language. The presence of qualifying words indicates that the author is taking special care with his or her words, which is certainly important when composing the right answer. After all, there are many ways to be wrong, but there is only one way to be right! For this reason, it is wise to avoid answers that are absolute when taking a multiple-choice test. An absolute answer is one that says things are either all one way or all another. They often include words like *every, always, best*, and *never*. If you are taking a multiple-choice test in a subject that doesn't lend itself to absolute answers, be on your guard if you see any of these words.

12. Long Answers

In many subject areas, the answers are not simple. As already mentioned, the right answer often requires hedges. Another common feature of the answers to a complex or subjective question are qualifying clauses, which are groups of words that subtly modify the meaning of the sentence. If the question or answer choice describes a rule to which there are exceptions or the subject matter is complicated, ambiguous, or confusing, the correct answer will require many words in order to be expressed clearly and accurately. In essence, you should not be deterred by answer choices that seem excessively long. Oftentimes, the author of the text will not be able to write the correct answer without

offering some qualifications and modifications. Your job is to read the answer choices thoroughly and completely and to select the one that most accurately and precisely answers the question.

13. Restating to Understand

Sometimes, a question on a multiple-choice test is difficult not because of what it asks but because of how it is written. If this is the case, restate the question or answer choice in different words. This process serves a couple of important purposes. First, it forces you to concentrate on the core of the question. In order to rephrase the question accurately, you have to understand it well. Rephrasing the question will concentrate your mind on the key words and ideas. Second, it will present the information to your mind in a fresh way. This process may trigger your memory and render some useful scrap of information picked up while studying.

14. True Statements

Sometimes an answer choice will be true in itself, but it does not answer the question. This is one of the main reasons why it is essential to read the question carefully and completely before proceeding to the answer choices. Too often, test takers skip ahead to the answer choices and look for true statements. Having found one of these, they are content to select it without reference to the question above. Obviously, this provides an easy way for test makers to play tricks. The savvy test taker will always read the entire question before turning to the answer choices. Then, having settled on a correct answer choice, he or she will refer to the original question and ensure that the selected answer is relevant. The mistake of choosing a correct-but-irrelevant answer choice is especially common on questions related to specific pieces of objective knowledge. A prepared test taker will have a wealth of factual knowledge at his or her disposal, and should not be careless in its application.

15. No Patterns

One of the more dangerous ideas that circulates about multiple-choice tests is that the correct answers tend to fall into patterns. These erroneous ideas range from a belief that B and C are the most common right answers, to the idea that an unprepared test-taker should answer "A-B-A-C-A-D-A-B-A." It cannot be emphasized enough that pattern-seeking of this type is exactly the WRONG way to approach a multiple-choice test. To begin with, it is highly unlikely that the test maker will plot the correct answers according to some predetermined pattern. The questions are scrambled and delivered in a random order. Furthermore, even if the test maker was following a pattern in the assignation of correct answers, there is no reason why the test taker would know which pattern he or she was using. Any attempt to discern a pattern in the answer choices is a waste of time and a distraction from the real work of taking the test. A test taker would be much better served by extra preparation before the test than by reliance on a pattern in the answers.

FREE DVD OFFER

Don't forget that doing well on your exam includes both understanding the test content and understanding how to use what you know to do well on the test. We offer a completely FREE Test Taking Tips DVD that covers world class test taking tips that you can use to be even more successful when you are taking your test.

All that we ask is that you email us your feedback about your study guide. To get your **FREE Test Taking Tips DVD**, email freedvd@studyguideteam.com with "FREE DVD" in the subject line and the following information in the body of the email:

- The title of your study guide.
- Your product rating on a scale of 1-5, with 5 being the highest rating.
- Your feedback about the study guide. What did you think of it?
- Your full name and shipping address to send your free DVD.

Introduction to the GRE

Function of the Test

The **Graduate Record Examination** (GRE) General Test is a standardized test administered by the Educational Testing Service (ETS) and used as part of the admissions process by masters, doctoral, and business programs at various universities. Specifically, the test is accepted or required by virtually every graduate and business program in the United States, as well as many schools around the world. There are also seven GRE tests in specific subject areas, but "GRE" in common usage refers only to the General Test.

In recent years, around 500,000 people have taken the GRE annually. Because the GRE is exclusively used as an admissions exam, most test takers are seniors in undergraduate programs who are planning to attend graduate school or college graduates who are seeking a graduate degree.

Test Administration

In the United States, the GRE is administered by computer, year-round at Prometric testing centers and, from time to time, on specific dates at other testing centers. In the typical middle-sized city, a location to take the test will be available somewhere in town on most days of any given month. Outside the U.S., the GRE is administered by computer or, where computer-testing sites are not available, by paper.

The fee for taking the GRE is the same worldwide, with the exception of China, where fees are slightly higher. The computer-based version of the test can be taken up to five times within any rolling twelve-month window, although test takers must wait at least 21 days after an attempt to retake the exam. Note, however, that individual schools' rules about how they treat retest scores may vary. Reasonable accommodations are available for test takers with disabilities, provided requests are submitted to, and approved by, ETS before the test taker schedules a test date. Requests may be made through the test taker's electronic account with ETS.

Test Format

The computer-based GRE is "adaptive by section," meaning that the difficulty of the second verbal and second quantitative sections that the test taker receives will depend on the his or her performance on the first of such sections completed. Test takers will have access to an on-screen calculator and may not use one of their own. Some questions provide multiple-choice answers, while others require test takers to fill-in-the-blank.

The total test time is around 3 hours and 45 minutes, broken down as follows:

Section	Time	Description
Analytical Writing	60 minutes	Two 30-minute "issue" and "argument" writing tasks
Verbal Reasoning	2 30-minute sections	20 questions assessing reading comprehension, critical reasoning, and vocabulary usage
Quantitative Reasoning	2 35-minute sections	20 questions assessing quantitative comparisons, problem solving items, and data interpretation questions
Experimental/Research Section	1 30- or 35-minute unscored section	May be either Verbal Reasoning or Quantitative Reasoning

Scoring

On the Verbal and Quantitative Reasoning sections, students receive a raw score that is simply the total number of questions answered correctly. There is no penalty for guessing. The raw score is then scaled to a score that ranges from 130 to 170. This score is available upon completion of the test.

There is no set "passing" score on the GRE; rather, each school considers test takers' scores relative to the school's standards and to the scores of other applicants. The average score on the test is between 150 and 152, while average scores for applicants for elite programs might be around 160.

The writing sections are scored later, on a scale from 0 to 6 in 0.5 point increments. The average score is around a 3.5.

Recent and Future Developments

The GRE has undergone major revisions over the years, most recently with the introduction of the current "GRE revised" test in 2011. Prior to that revision, the test was adaptive from question to question (rather than from section to section) and was scored on a 1600-point scale. No substantial changes have been announced recently.

Verbal Reasoning

The **Verbal Reasoning** sections test a reader's ability to evaluate writing based on the logical development of points and sub-points, analyze and evaluate increasingly complex concepts, and understand the relationships of parts of the reading material to the whole in order to make comprehensive and meaningful sense out of texts. Therefore, it is wise for the reader to use several different study strategies to prepare for successful results when taking the Verbal Reasoning portion of the GRE exam.

Overall Question Structure

Several question structures are presented in the test. For example, in **Reading Comprehension**, test takers will be asked to read paragraphs and then will be presented with questions and possible answers that best support the meaning of the text. Another question structure, **Text Completion**, presents a statement with missing words. The reader will be asked to supply vocabulary words from a provided list to clarify the meaning of the sentence. The final question structure, **Sentence Equivalence**, is a single sentence with a missing word. The reader will select the two best possible missing words from a list of vocabulary words.

Reading and Vocabulary Preparation

The GRE Verbal Reasoning Exam tests one's ability to identify words used in context. Therefore, one of the best strategies for preparing for the test is to read high-level material. As one reads, he or she should highlight challenging vocabulary words and write down the words and definitions on a separate document or on flashcards to review during the preparation stage. Because of effective reading preparation, the reader may have stronger recall during the test when he or she comes across a word that is confusing. Readers must try to remember whether the word was used in a positive context or a negative context in their previous reading. This may help the reader make an educated guess during the test. Finally, as one studies word lists for the GRE, he or she should remember that the text completion and the sentence equivalence questions rely on understanding the words in context; therefore, it would be helpful for test takers to study synonyms and antonyms of vocabulary words.

Regarding the sentences in the GRE, note that the topics range from history to literature to geography. Test takers should read the sentences for cue words that will help determine the main idea the writer intended for the sentence as a whole and make relationships between the words selected in the sentence to the developing theme.

Reading Comprehension

Question Format

The GRE Reading Comprehension exercises vary in length from one to several paragraphs. Typically, shorter passages have one or two response questions, while longer passages have one to five associated questions.

First, one should read the passage carefully and look for clues as to how the development of the text completes the understanding of the paragraph. Signal words help determine the author's full intent. For example, the words *like*, *moreover*, *although*, and *alternately* imply a comparison or contrast.

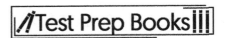

Additionally, one should read thoroughly in order to understand the author's logic and to recall the significant points developed in the passage.

Multiple-Choice: Choose One Answer Choice

Readers will be faced with multiple-choice questions where they must pick one single answer. They should evaluate each multiple-choice question carefully before responding. The following are suggestions for readers who are faced with choosing one answer choice:

- Readers should carefully review all of the options before selecting an answer. Ideas that are introduced in the choice selection (and therefore are not presented or inferred in the passage) are not an appropriate answer option. One should read each answer choice slowly to decide whether or not it relates to the question.

- Readers should select the answer that is the best possible option. Other choices may seem reasonable, but readers must select the option that works best within the context of the information presented. It is wise for readers to take their time and to digest all the choices before making their selection.

- If a reader is not sure which option to choose, he or she should return to the main point of the question. Readers should try to select the answer option that fits the best with the information provided in the question and not get distracted by information beyond the selection in question. If readers have to return to the passage for more clues, they should read key points instead of the entire selection to keep within the time frame given.

Multiple-Choice: Choose One or More Answer Choices

Readers might be faced with questions where they will have to choose all the correct answers from a list of three options. The answer may include one, two, or all three options. Readers must select all the correct answers to receive a positive score. Suggestions for this question format include the following:

- Readers can try to come up with correct answers before the answer options are read. That way, off-based answer options can quickly be eliminated. Rather than seeking connections between the options, each choice can be read with respect to the question. If a choice has a relationship to the question, test takers should mark it as a correct choice while they further consider other options.

- Readers should avoid rushing through the selection process. Instead, they should carefully select all the responses that work, whether that includes one, two, or three options. If readers make a rushed decision, they may miss the subtle ways that the author aligns the answers specifically to see if readers have used critical thinking strategies. Readers should practice using all their reading comprehension strategies before selecting choices.

Practice Examples

Questions 1–3 are based on this passage:

Most notably rooted in the Black musical experience, jazz music has been hailed as a true American art form. Responding to the late nineteenth- and twentieth-century influence of both European American and African American musical history, jazz music as a developing genre, originating from pocket neighborhoods of New Orleans, offered a combination of traditional and popular musical influences. For over one hundred years, jazz incorporated the popular performance sounds of swing, improvisation, double discordant rhythms, and offbeat sounds. There are echoes of blues, big band sounds, and ragtime in the popular sounds of American jazz. During the jazz music evolution, other cultures added their musical styles to create a rich variety of subgenres, and later, fusion genres. The jazz musician's ability to improvise and use sounds to convey meaning offered a unique form of creative communication between the music maker and the listener. Because women jazz singers such as Billie Holiday and Ella Fitzgerald, and piano players like Lil Hardin Armstrong, attracted the applause of American audiences, the role of women gained a recognizable measure of social acceptance dating back to the 1920s. During the years of Prohibition in the United States, speakeasies furthered the jazz age culture of music, song, and dance, especially among the younger generation. Free jazz—a style of jazz that loosened the reins of meter, beat, and symmetry rules—was made popular by John Coltrane in the 1960s. Many other jazz styles emerged over the years including bebop—a musically challenging form of jazz; cool jazz—a Miles Davis favorite, noted for using long melody lines for a calming effect; soul jazz—taking some sounds from old gospel music; and smooth jazz—an early 1980s pop form of jazz. Finally, with the emergence of electronic music, jazz-rock music gained popularity in the early 2000s. Jazz will go down in history as a truly authentic American art form.

Select only one best answer choice.

1. Based on the information from the passage, which statement can be inferred to be true about the role of women and jazz?
   a. Women were not allowed to perform in American establishments where alcohol was served, which limited the success of female jazz singers and musicians during the 1920s.
   b. In the 1960s, women jazz singers and musicians first began to gain recognition as talented jazz entertainers, which garnered social recognition for them and subsequently gave them a respected place in American society.
   c. Billie Holiday and Ella Fitzgerald were members of an all-women jazz singing group; these all-female singing groups became popular because many of the men were enlisted in the armed forces during the wartime years.
   d. Female jazz artists, including both singers and jazz piano players, gained respect from American audiences long before the popular smooth jazz period emerged in the 1980s.
   e. European audiences accepted women jazz musicians because it was widely acknowledged that improvising skills, a trademark of jazz music, were more suited to the emotional makeup of women than men.

Explanation:

Choice *D* is correct based on the sentence that reads, "Because women jazz singers like Billie Holiday and Ella Fitzgerald, and piano players like Lil Hardin Armstrong, attracted the applause of American audiences, the role of women gained a recognizable measure of social acceptance dating back to the 1920s." Choice *A* is incorrect because there is no mention of the women being allowed or not allowed in an establishment that served alcohol. Choice *B* is incorrect because the passage clearly states that the role of women and jazz was appealing to American audiences as early as the 1920s. Choice *C* is incorrect because the passage does not indicate that Billie Holiday and Ella Fitzgerald were members of an all-women jazz group. Choice *E* is incorrect because there is no statement in the passage regarding a connection between jazz music and the emotional makeup of women.

Consider each of the choices separately and select all that apply:

2. The passage suggests that jazz music, in all its forms, constitutes an authentic American art form for which of the following reasons?
   a. Jazz music emerged from small neighborhoods of New Orleans and preserved the basic features of purely traditional jazz sounds.
   b. Jazz music borrowed sounds from nineteenth- and twentieth-century European and African American musical history, which influenced the way jazz music evolved.
   c. Jazz music keeps its musical traditions consistent because, within the evolution of jazz music, there was never a time when meter, beat, and symmetry rules were dropped.
   d. During the jazz music evolution, other cultures added their musical styles to create a rich variety of subgenres, and later, fusion genres.
   e. Jazz musicians enjoyed improvising and using unique and creative sounds to convey meaning and communicate messages to the audience.

Explanation:

Choices *B*, *D*, and *E* are correct because the passage states that all three points contributed to the evolution of jazz music as an authentic American art form. Choice *A* is incorrect because it is only partially true; jazz music also borrowed sounds from popular music, not just traditional sounds. Choice *C* is incorrect because the passage states that free jazz loosened the rules of meter, beat, and symmetry.

Consider each of the choices separately and select all that apply:

3. According to the passage, which statements are accurate regarding the jazz artists and the time period when their jazz style was popularized?
   a. Miles Davis was a favorite cool jazz player; he became popular for improvising with long melody lines, which gave the music a calming effect.
   b. Ella Fitzgerald was not a pianist, but her voice had deep, rich tones, which gained her acceptance with American audiences.
   c. Billie Holiday was both a jazz singer and a jazz piano player who was popular with both European and American audiences.
   d. John Coltrane created edgy sounds by dropping the rules of meter, beat, and symmetry. His jazz music was popularized during the 1960s and fell into the "free jazz" category.
   e. There are obvious sounds of blues, big band, and ragtime in the developing art of jazz music, which is another reason that jazz became known as authentic American music.

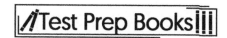

Explanation:

Choices *A* and *D* are correct based on the passage that states that Miles Davis became popular with cool jazz and John Coltrane loosened the rules of meter, beat, and symmetry. Choice *B* is incorrect because while it might be factually true, it contains details that are not stated in the passage. The choice mentions the "deep, rich tones" of Ella Fitzgerald's voice being the reason she gained acceptance with American audiences, but support of this assertion is not found in the passage; therefore, it is just a conjecture. Choice *C* is incorrect because the passage does not claim that Billie Holiday was both a jazz singer and a jazz pianist, nor does it note the role of European audiences in her popularity. Choice *E* is incorrect because although the passage states that "there are echoes of blues, big band sounds, and ragtime in the popular sounds of American jazz," the question asks for statements that are true regarding jazz artists and the time period when their jazz style was popularized, and this answer choice is instead talking about the qualities that make jazz is authentic American music. Therefore, Choice *E* is not a viable answer to this question since it is about neither jazz artists nor the time period when their jazz style was popularized.

Central Ideas and Details

Topic, Main Idea, Supporting Details, and Themes
The **topic** of a text is the overall subject, and the **main idea** more specifically builds on that subject. Consider a paragraph that begins with the following: "The United States government is made of up three branches: executive, judicial, and legislative." If this sentence is divided into its essential components, there is the topic (United States Government) and the main idea (the three branches of government).

A main idea must be supported with details, which usually appear in the form of quotations, paraphrasing, or analysis. Authors should connect details and analysis to the main point. Readers should always be cautious when accepting the validity of an argument and look for logical fallacies, such as slippery slope, straw man, and begging the question. It's okay for a reader to disagree with an author, because arguments may seem sound, but further analysis often reveals they are flawed.

It is important to remember that when most authors write, they want to make a point or send a message. This point, or the message of a text, is known as the **theme**. Authors may state themes explicitly, like in *Aesop's Fables*. More often, especially in modern literature, readers must infer the theme based on textual details. Usually, after carefully reading and analyzing an entire text, the theme emerges. Typically, the longer the piece, the more numerous its themes, though often one theme dominates the rest, as evidenced by the author's purposeful revisiting of it throughout the passage.

Cultural Differences in Themes
Regardless of culture, place, or time, certain themes are universal to the human condition. Because all humans experience certain feelings and engage in similar experiences—birth, death, marriage, friendship, finding meaning, etc.—certain themes span cultures. However, different cultures have different norms and general beliefs concerning these themes. For example, the theme of maturing and crossing from childhood to adulthood is a global theme; however, the literature from one culture might imply that this happens in someone's twenties, while another culture's literature might imply that it happens in the early teenage years.

It's important for the reader to be aware of these differences. Readers must avoid being **ethnocentric**, which means believing the aspects of one's own culture to be superior to those of other cultures.

Analyzing Topics and Summary Sentences

Good writers get to the point quickly. This is accomplished by developing a strong and effective topic sentence that details the author's purpose and answers questions such as *What does the author intend to explain or impress?* or *What does the author want the reader to believe?* The **topic sentence** is normally found at the beginning of a supporting paragraph and usually gives purpose to a single paragraph. Critical readers should find the topic sentence in each paragraph. If all information points back to one sentence, it's the topic sentence.

Summary sentences offer a recap of previously discussed information before transitioning to the next point or proceeding to the closing thoughts. Summary sentences can be found at the end of supporting paragraphs and in the conclusion of a text.

Identifying Logical Conclusions

Determining conclusions requires being an active reader, as a reader must make a prediction and analyze facts to identify a conclusion. A reader should identify key words in a passage to determine the logical conclusion from the information presented. Consider the passage below:

> Lindsay, covered in flour, moved around the kitchen frantically. Her mom yelled from another room, "Lindsay, we're going to be late!"

Readers can conclude that Lindsay's next steps are to finish baking, clean herself up, and head off somewhere with her baked goods. It's important to note that the conclusion cannot be verified factually. Many conclusions are not spelled out specifically in the text; thus, they have to be inferred and deduced by the reader.

Evaluating a Passage

Readers draw **conclusions** about what an author has presented. This helps them better understand what the writer has intended to communicate and whether they agree with what the author has offered. There are a few ways to determine a logical conclusion, but careful reading is the most important. It's helpful to read a passage a few times, noting details that seem important to the piece. Sometimes, readers arrive at a conclusion that is different than what the writer intended, or they may come up with more than one conclusion.

Textual evidence within the details helps readers draw a conclusion about a passage. **Textual evidence** refers to information—facts and examples—that support the main point. Textual evidence will likely come from outside sources and can be in the form of quoted or paraphrased material. In order to draw a conclusion from evidence, it's important to examine the credibility and validity of that evidence as well as how (and if) it relates to the main idea.

If an author presents a differing opinion or a **counterargument**, in order to refute it, the reader should consider how and why this information is being presented. It is meant to strengthen the original argument and shouldn't be confused with the author's intended conclusion, but it should also be considered in the reader's final evaluation.

Sometimes, authors explicitly state the conclusion that they want readers to understand. Alternatively, a conclusion may not be directly stated. In that case, readers must rely on the implications to form a logical conclusion:

> On the way to the bus stop, Michael realized his homework wasn't in his backpack. He ran back to the house to get it and made it back to the bus just in time.

In this example, although it's never explicitly stated, it can be inferred that Michael is a student on his way to school in the morning. When forming a conclusion from implied information, it's important to read the text carefully to find several pieces of evidence to support the conclusion.

Summarizing is an effective way to draw a conclusion from a passage. A **summary** is a shortened version of the original text, written by the reader in his or her own words. Focusing on the main points of the original text and including only the relevant details can help readers reach a conclusion. It's important to retain the original meaning of the passage.

Like summarizing, **paraphrasing** can also help a reader fully understand different parts of a text. Paraphrasing calls for the reader to take a small part of the passage and list or describe its main points. However, paraphrasing is more than rewording the original passage; it should be written in the reader's own words, while still retaining the meaning of the original source. This will indicate an understanding of the original source, yet still help the reader expand on his or her interpretation.

Structure of Text

Word and Phrase Meanings

Most experts agree that learning new words is worth the time it takes. It helps readers understand what they are reading, and it expands their vocabulary. An extensive vocabulary improves one's ability to think. When words are added to someone's vocabulary, he or she is better able to make sense of the world.

One of the fastest ways to decode a word is through context. **Context**, or surrounding words, gives clues as to what unknown words mean. Take the following example: *When the students in the classroom teased Johnny, he was so discombobulated that he couldn't finish a simple math problem.* Even though a reader might be unfamiliar with the word *discombobulated*, he or she can use context clues in the sentence to make sense of the word. In this case, it can be deduced that *discombobulated* means confused or distracted.

Although context clues provide a rudimentary understanding of a word, using a dictionary can provide the reader with a more comprehensive meaning of the word. Printed dictionaries list words in alphabetical order, and all versions—including those online—include a word's multiple meanings. Typically, the first definition is the most widely used or known. The second, third, and subsequent entries move toward the more unusual or archaic. Dictionaries also indicate the part(s) of speech of each word, such as noun, verb, adjective, etc.

Dictionaries are not fixed in time. The English language today looks nothing like it did in Shakespeare's time, and Shakespeare's English is vastly different from Chaucer's. The English language is constantly evolving, as evidenced by the deletion of old words and the addition of new ones. *Ginormous* and *bling-bling*, for example, can both be found in *Merriam-Webster's* latest edition, yet they were not found in prior editions.

Analyzing an Author's Rhetorical Choices

Authors utilize a wide range of techniques to tell a story or communicate information. Readers should be familiar with the most common of these techniques. Techniques of writing are also known as **rhetorical devices**.

In nonfiction writing, authors employ argumentative techniques to present their opinions to readers in the most convincing way. Persuasive writing usually includes at least one type of **appeal**: an appeal to logic (**logos**), emotion (**pathos**), or credibility and trustworthiness (**ethos**). When writers appeal to logic, they are asking readers to agree with them based on research, evidence, and an established line of reasoning. An author's argument might also appeal to readers' emotions, perhaps by including personal stories and **anecdotes** (a short narrative of a specific event). A final type of appeal—appeal to authority—asks the reader to agree with the author's argument on the basis of their expertise or credentials. Three different approaches to arguing the same opinion are exemplified below:

Logic (Logos)

Our school should abolish its current ban on cell phone use on campus. This rule was adopted last year as an attempt to reduce class disruptions and help students focus more on their lessons. However, since the rule was enacted, there has been no change in the number of disciplinary problems in class. Therefore, the rule is ineffective and should be done away with.

The above is an example of an appeal to logic. The author uses evidence to disprove the logic of the school's rule (the rule was supposed to reduce discipline problems, but the number of problems has not been reduced; therefore, the rule is not working) and to call for its repeal.

Emotion (Pathos)

An author's argument might also appeal to readers' emotions, perhaps by including personal stories and anecdotes.

The next example presents an appeal to emotion. By sharing the personal anecdote of one student and speaking about emotional topics like family relationships, the author invokes the reader's empathy in asking them to reconsider the school rule.

Our school should abolish its current ban on cell phone use on campus. If they aren't able to use their phones during the school day, many students feel isolated from their loved ones. For example, last semester, one student's grandmother had a heart attack in the morning. However, because he couldn't use his cell phone, the student didn't know about his grandmother's accident until the end of the day—when she had already passed away, and it was too late to say goodbye. By preventing students from contacting their friends and family, our school is placing undue stress and anxiety on students.

Credibility (Ethos)

Finally, an appeal to authority includes a statement from a relevant expert. In this case, the author uses a doctor in the field of education to support the argument. All three examples begin from the same opinion—the school's phone ban needs to change—but rely on different argumentative styles to persuade the reader.

Our school should abolish its current ban on cell phone use on campus. According to Dr. Bartholomew Everett, a leading educational expert, "Research studies show that cell phone usage has no real impact on student attentiveness. Rather, phones provide a valuable technological resource for learning. Schools need to learn how to integrate this new technology into their curriculum." Rather than banning phones altogether, our school should follow the advice of experts and allow students to use phones as part of their learning.

Rhetorical Questions

Another commonly used argumentative technique is asking **rhetorical questions**, which are questions that do not actually require an answer but that push the reader to consider the topic further.

I wholly disagree with the proposal to ban restaurants from serving foods with high sugar and sodium contents. Do we really want to live in a world where the government can control what we eat? I prefer to make my own food choices.

Here, the author's rhetorical question prompts readers to put themselves in a hypothetical situation and imagine how they would feel about it.

Figurative Language

Similes and **metaphors** are types of figurative language that are used as rhetorical devices. Both are comparisons between two things, but their formats differ slightly. A simile says that two things are similar and makes a comparison using "like" or "as"—A is like B, or A is as [some characteristic] as B—whereas a metaphor states that two things are exactly the same—A is B. In both cases, similes and metaphors invite the reader to think more deeply about the characteristics of the two subjects and consider where they overlap. Sometimes the poet develops a complex metaphor throughout the entire poem; this is known as an **extended metaphor**. An example of metaphor can be found in the sentence: "His pillow was a fluffy cloud." An example of simile can be found in the first line of Robert Burns' famous poem:

My love is like a red, red rose

This is comparison using "like," and the two things being compared are love and a rose. Some characteristics of a rose are that it is fragrant, beautiful, blossoming, colorful, vibrant—by comparing his love to a red, red rose, Burns asks the reader to apply these qualities of a rose to his love. In this way, he implies that his love is also fresh, blossoming, and brilliant.

Analyzing and Evaluating Text Structure

Depending on what the author is attempting to accomplish, certain formats or text structures work better than others. For example, a sequence structure might work for narration but not when identifying similarities and differences between dissimilar concepts. Similarly, a comparison-contrast structure is not useful for narration. It's the author's job to put the right information in the correct format.

Readers should be familiar with the five main literary structures:

1. **Sequence** structure (sometimes referred to as the order structure) is when the order of events proceeds in a predictable manner. In many cases, this means the text goes through the plot elements: exposition, rising action, climax, falling action, and resolution. Readers are introduced to

characters, setting, and conflict in the exposition. In the rising action, there's an increase in tension and suspense. The climax is the height of tension and the point of no return. Tension decreases during the falling action. In the resolution, any conflicts presented in the exposition are solved, and the story concludes. An informative text that is structured sequentially will often go in order from one step to the next.

2. In the **problem-solution** structure, authors identify a potential problem and suggest a solution. This form of writing is usually divided into two paragraphs and can be found in informational texts. For example, cell phone, cable, and satellite providers use this structure in manuals to help customers troubleshoot or identify problems with services or products.

3. When authors want to discuss similarities and differences between separate concepts, they arrange thoughts in a **comparison-contrast** paragraph structure. **Venn diagrams** are an effective graphic organizer for comparison-contrast structures because they feature two overlapping circles that can be used to organize and group similarities and differences. A comparison-contrast essay organizes one paragraph based on similarities and another based on differences. A comparison-contrast essay can also be arranged with the similarities and differences of individual traits addressed within individual paragraphs. Words such as *however*, *but*, and *nevertheless* help signal a contrast in ideas.

4. The **descriptive** writing structure is designed to appeal to one's senses. Much like an artist who constructs a painting, good descriptive writing builds an image in the reader's mind by appealing to the five senses: sight, hearing, taste, touch, and smell. However, overly descriptive writing can become tedious; whereas sparse descriptions can make settings and characters seem flat. Good authors strike a balance by applying descriptions only to passages, characters, and settings that are integral to the plot.

5. Passages that use the **cause and effect** structure are simply asking *why* by demonstrating some type of connection between ideas. Words such as *if*, *since*, *because*, *then*, or *consequently* indicate relationship. By switching the order of a complex sentence, the writer can rearrange the emphasis on different clauses. Saying *If Sheryl is late, we'll miss the dance* is different from saying, *We'll miss the dance if Sheryl is late*. One emphasizes Sheryl's tardiness while the other emphasizes missing the dance. Paragraphs can also be arranged in a cause and effect format. Since the format—before and after—is sequential, it is useful when authors wish to discuss the impact of choices. Researchers often apply this paragraph structure to the scientific method.

Authorial Purpose and Perspective

No matter the genre or format, all authors are writing to persuade, inform, entertain, or express feelings. Often, these purposes are blended, with one dominating the rest. It's useful to learn to recognize the author's intent.

Persuasive writing is used to persuade or convince readers of something. It often contains two elements: the argument and the counterargument. The **argument** takes a stance on an issue, while the **counterargument** pokes holes in the opposition's stance. Authors rely on logic, emotion, and writer credibility to persuade readers to agree with them. If readers are opposed to the stance before reading, they are unlikely to adopt that stance. However, those who are undecided or committed to the same stance are more likely to agree with the author.

Informative writing tries to teach or inform. Workplace manuals, instructor lessons, statistical reports and cookbooks are examples of informative texts. Informative writing is usually based on facts and is often without emotion and persuasion. Informative texts generally contain statistics, charts, and graphs. Although most informative texts lack a persuasive agenda, readers must examine the text carefully to determine whether one exists within a given passage.

Stories or **narratives** are designed to entertain. When people go to the movies, they often want to escape for a few hours, not necessarily to think critically. **Entertaining** writing is designed to delight and engage the reader. However, sometimes this type of writing can be woven into more serious materials, such as persuasive or informative writing, to hook the reader before transitioning into a more scholarly discussion.

Emotional writing works to evoke the reader's feelings, such as anger, euphoria, or sadness. The connection between reader and author is an attempt to cause the reader to share the author's intended emotion or tone. Sometimes, in order to make a text more poignant, the author simply wants readers to feel the emotions that the author has felt. Other times, the author attempts to persuade or manipulate the reader into adopting their stance. While it's okay to sympathize with the author, readers should be aware of the individual's underlying intent.

Point of View

Point of view is another important writing device to consider. In fiction writing, **point of view** refers to who tells the story or from whose perspective readers are observing the story. In nonfiction writing, the **point of view** refers to whether the author refers to himself or herself, his or her readers, or chooses not to mention either. Whether fiction or nonfiction, the author carefully considers the impact the perspective will have on the purpose and main point of the writing.

- **First-person** point of view: The story is told from the writer's perspective. In fiction, this would mean that the main character is also the narrator. First-person point of view is easily recognized by the use of personal pronouns such as *I, me, we, us, our, my*, and *myself*.

- **Third-person** point of view: In a more formal essay, this would be an appropriate perspective because the focus should be on the subject matter, not the writer or the reader. Third-person point of view is recognized by the use of the pronouns *he, she, they*, and *it*. In fiction writing, third-person point of view has a few variations.

    - **Third-person limited** point of view refers to a story told by a narrator who has access to the thoughts and feelings of just one character.

    - In **third-person omniscient** point of view, the narrator has access to the thoughts and feelings of all the characters.

    - In **third-person objective** point of view, the narrator is like a fly on the wall and can see and hear what the characters do and say but does not have access to their thoughts and feelings.

- **Second-person** point of view: This point of view isn't commonly used in fiction or nonfiction writing because it directly addresses the reader using the pronouns *you, your*, and *yourself*. Second-person perspective is more appropriate in direct communication, such as business letters or emails.

Point of View	Pronouns used
First person	I, me, we, us, our, my, myself
Second person	You, your, yourself
Third person	He, she, it, they

Interpreting Authorial Decisions Rhetorically

There are a few ways for readers to engage actively with the text, such as making inferences and predictions. An **inference** refers to a point that is implied (as opposed to directly-stated) by the evidence presented:

> Bradley packed up all of the items from his desk in a box and said goodbye to his coworkers for the last time.

From this sentence, although it is not directly stated, readers can infer that Bradley is leaving his job. It's necessary to use inference in order to draw conclusions about the meaning of a passage. When making an inference about a passage, it's important to rely only on the information that is provided in the text itself. This helps readers ensure that their conclusions are valid.

Readers will also find themselves making predictions when reading a passage or paragraph. **Predictions** are guesses about what's going to happen next. This is a natural tendency, especially when reading a good story or watching a suspenseful movie. It's fun to try to figure out how it will end. Authors intentionally use suspenseful language and situations to keep readers interested:

> A cat darted across the street just as the car came careening around the curve.

One unfortunate prediction might be that the car will hit the cat. Of course, predictions aren't always accurate, so it's important to read carefully to the end of the text to determine the accuracy of one's predictions.

Readers should pay attention to the **sequence**, or the order in which details are laid out in the text, as this can be important to understanding its meaning as a whole. Writers will often use transitional words to help the reader understand the order of events and to stay on track. Words like *next, then, after*, and *finally* show that the order of events is important to the author. In some cases, the author omits these transitional words, and the sequence is implied. Authors may even purposely present the information out of order to make an impact or have an effect on the reader. An example might be when a narrative writer uses **flashback** to reveal information.

Drawing conclusions is also important when actively reading a passage. **Hedge phrases** such as *will, might, probably*, and *appear to be* are used by writers who want to cover their bases and show there are exceptions to their statements. **Absolute phrasing**, such as *always* and *never*, should be carefully considered, as the use of these words and their intended meanings are often incorrect.

Identifying the Appropriate Source for Locating Information

With a wealth of information at people's fingertips in this digital age, it's important to know not only the type of information one is looking for, but also in what medium he or she is most likely to find it. Information needs to be specific and reliable. For example, if someone is repairing a car, an encyclopedia would be mostly useless. While an encyclopedia might include information about cars, an owner's manual will contain the specific information needed for repairs. Information must also be reliable or credible so that it can be trusted. A well-known newspaper may have reliable information,

but a peer-reviewed journal article will have likely gone through a more rigorous check for validity. Determining **bias** can be helpful in determining credibility. If the information source (person, organization, or company) has something to gain from the reader forming a certain view on a topic, it's likely the information is skewed. For example, if trying to find the unemployment rate, the Bureau of Labor Statistics is a more credible source than a politician's speech.

Primary sources are best defined as records or items that serve as evidence of periods of history. To be considered primary, the source documents or objects must have been created during the time period in which they reference. Examples include diaries, newspaper articles, speeches, government documents, photographs, and historical artifacts. In today's digital age, primary sources, which were once in print, are often embedded in secondary sources. **Secondary sources**—such as websites, history books, databases, or reviews—contain analysis or commentary on primary sources. Secondary sources borrow information from primary sources through the process of quoting, summarizing, or paraphrasing.

Today's students often complete research online through **electronic sources**. Electronic sources offer advantages over print, and can be accessed on virtually any computer, while libraries or other research centers are limited to fixed locations and specific catalogs. Electronic sources are also efficient and yield massive amounts of data in seconds. The user can tailor a search based on key words, publication years, and article length. Lastly, many **databases** provide the user with instant citations, saving the user the trouble of manually assembling sources for a bibliography.

Although electronic sources yield powerful results, researchers must use caution. While there are many reputable and reliable sources on the internet, just as many are unreliable or biased sources. It's up to the researcher to examine and verify the reliability of sources. *Wikipedia*, for example, may or may not be accurate, depending on the contributor. Many databases, such as *EBSCO* or *SIRS*, offer peer-reviewed articles, meaning the publications have been reviewed for the quality and accuracy of their content.

Integration of Ideas

Understanding Authors' Claims

The goal of most persuasive and informative texts is to make a claim and support it with evidence. A **claim** is a statement made as though it is fact. Many claims are opinions; for example, "stealing is wrong." While this is generally true, it is arguable, meaning it is capable of being challenged. An initial reaction to "stealing is wrong" might be to agree; however, there may be circumstances in which it is warranted. If it is necessary for the survival of an individual or their loved ones (i.e., if they are starving and cannot afford to eat), then this assertion becomes morally ambiguous. While it may still be illegal, whether it is "wrong" is unclear.

When an assertion is made within a text, it is typically reinforced with supporting details as is exemplified in the following passage:

> The extinction of the dinosaurs has been a hot debate amongst scientists since the discovery of fossils in the eighteenth century. Numerous theories were developed in explanation, including extreme climate change, an epidemic of disease, or changes in the atmosphere. It wasn't until the late 1970s that a young geochemist, named Walter Alvarez, noticed significant changes in the soil layers of limestone he was studying in Italy. The layers contained fossilized remains of millions of small organisms within the layer that corresponded with the same period in which the dinosaurs lived. He noticed that the soil layer directly above this layer was suddenly devoid of any trace of these

organisms. The soil layer directly above *this* layer was filled with an entirely new species of organisms. It seemed the first species had disappeared at the exact same time as the dinosaurs!

With the help of his father, Walter Alvarez analyzed the soil layer between the extinct species and the new species and realized this layer was filled with an abnormal amount of *iridium*—a substance that is abundant in meteorites but almost never found on Earth. Unlike other elements in the fossil record, which take a long time to deposit, the iridium had been laid down very abruptly. The layer also contained high levels of soot, enough to account for all of the earth's forests burning to the ground at the same time. This led scientists to create the best-supported theory that the tiny organisms, as well as the dinosaurs and countless other species, had been destroyed by a giant asteroid that had slammed into Earth, raining tons of iridium down on the planet from a giant cosmic cloud.

Supporting Claims

Before embarking on answering these questions, readers should summarize each. This will help in locating the supporting evidence. These summaries can be written down or completed mentally; full sentences are not necessary.

Paragraph 1: Layer of limestone shows that a species of organisms disappeared at same time as the dinosaurs.

Paragraph 2: Layer had high amounts of iridium and soot—scientists believe dinosaurs destroyed by asteroid.

Simply by summarizing the text, it has been plainly outlined where there will be answers to relevant questions. Although there are often claims already embedded within an educational text, a claim will most likely be given, but the evidence to support it will need to be located. Take this example question:

> Q: What evidence within the text best supports the theory that the dinosaurs became extinct because of an asteroid?

The claim here is that the <u>dinosaurs went extinct because of an asteroid</u>. Because the text is already outlined in the summaries, it is easy to see that the evidence supporting this theory is in the second paragraph:

> With the help of his father, they analyzed the soil layer between the extinct species and the new species and realized <u>this layer was filled with an abnormal amount of *iridium*</u>— a substance that is <u>abundant is meteorites</u> but almost never found on Earth. Unlike other elements in the fossil record, which takes a long time to deposit, the iridium had been laid down very abruptly. <u>The layer also contained high levels of soot</u>, enough to account for all of the earth's forests burning to the ground at the same time. <u>This led scientists to create the best-supported theory</u> that the tiny organisms, as well as the dinosaurs and countless other species, had been <u>destroyed by a giant asteroid</u> that had slammed into Earth, <u>raining tons of iridium down on the planet</u> from a giant cosmic cloud.

Now that the evidence within the text that best supports the theory has been located, the answer choices can be evaluated:

    a. Changes in climate and atmosphere caused an asteroid to crash into Earth

    b. Walter and Luis Alvarez studied limestone with fossilized organisms

    c. A soil layer lacking organisms that existed at the same time as the dinosaurs showed low levels of iridium

    d. A soil layer lacking organisms that existed at the same time as the dinosaurs showed high levels of iridium

Answer choice (a) is clearly false as there is nothing within the text that claims that climate changes caused an asteroid to crash into Earth. This kind of answer choice displays an incorrect use of detail. Although the passage may have contained the words "change," "climate," and "atmosphere," these terms were manipulated to form an erroneous answer.

Answer choice (b) is incorrect because while the scientists did study limestone with fossilized organisms, and in doing so they discovered evidence that led to the formation of the theory, this is not the actual evidence itself. This is an example of an out-of-scope answer choice: a true statement that may or may not have been in the passage, but that isn't the whole answer or isn't the point.

Answer choice (c) is incorrect because it is the opposite of the correct answer. Assuming the second paragraph was summarized correctly, it is already known that the soil layer contained *high* levels of iridium, not low levels. Even if the paragraph was not summarized that way, the final sentence states that "tons of iridium rained down on the planet." So, answer choice (c) is false.

Answer choice (d) is correct because it matches the evidence found in the second paragraph.

Fact and Opinion, Biases, and Stereotypes

It is important to distinguish between facts and opinions when reading a piece of writing. When an author presents **facts**, such as statistics or data, readers should be able to check those facts to verify that they are accurate. When authors share their own thoughts and feelings about a subject, they are expressing their **opinions**.

Authors often use words like *think, feel, believe,* or *in my opinion* when expressing an opinion, but these words won't always appear in an opinion piece, especially if it is formally written. An author's opinion may be backed up by facts, which gives it more credibility, but that opinion should not be taken as fact. A critical reader should be suspect of an author's opinion, especially if it is only supported by other opinions.

Fact	Opinion
There are nine innings in a game of baseball.	Baseball games run too long.
James Garfield was assassinated on July 2, 1881.	James Garfield was a good president.
McDonald's® has stores in 118 countries.	McDonald's® has the best hamburgers.

Critical readers examine the facts used to support an author's argument. They check the facts against other sources to be sure those facts are correct. They also check the validity of the sources used to be sure those sources are credible, academic, and/or peer-reviewed. When an author uses another person's opinion to support his or her argument, even if it is an expert's opinion, it is still only an opinion and should not be taken as fact. A strong argument uses valid, measurable facts to support ideas. Even then, the reader may disagree with the argument.

An authoritative argument may use facts to sway the reader. For example, many experts differ in their opinions on whether or not homework should be assigned to elementary school students. Because of this, a writer may choose to only use the information and experts' opinions that supports their viewpoint. If the argument is that homework is necessary for reinforcing lessons taught in class, the author will use facts that support this idea. That same author may leave out relevant facts on excessive amounts of homework having a negative impact on grades and students' attitudes towards learning. The way the author uses facts can influence the reader, so it's important to consider the facts being used, how those facts are being presented, and what information might be left out.

Authors can also demonstrate **bias** if they ignore an opposing viewpoint or present their side in an unbalanced way. A strong argument considers the opposition and finds a way to refute it. Critical readers should look for an unfair or one-sided presentation of the argument and be skeptical, as a bias may be present. Even if this bias is unintentional, if it exists in the writing, the reader should be wary of the validity of the argument.

Readers should also look for the use of stereotypes that refer to specific groups. **Stereotypes** are often negative connotations about a person or place and should always be avoided. When a critical reader finds stereotypes in a piece of writing, he or she should immediately be critical of the argument and consider the validity of anything the author presents. Stereotypes reveal a flaw in the writer's thinking and may suggest a lack of knowledge or understanding about the subject.

Using Evidence to Make Connections Between Different Texts

When analyzing two or more texts, there are several different aspects that need to be considered, particularly the styles (or the artful way in which the authors use diction to deliver a theme), points of view, and types of argument. In order to do so, one should compare and contrast the following elements between the texts:

- Style: narrative, persuasive, descriptive, informative, etc.
- Tone: sarcastic, angry, somber, humorous, etc.
- Sentence structure: simple (1 clause) compound (2 clauses), complex-compound (3 clauses)
- Punctuation choice: question marks, exclamation points, periods, dashes, etc.
- Point of view: first person, second person, third person
- Paragraph structure: long, short, both, differences between the two
- Organizational structure: compare/contrast, problem/solution, chronological, etc.

The following two passages concern the theme of death and are presented to demonstrate how to evaluate the above elements:

Passage I

Death occurs in several stages. The first stage is the pre-active stage, which occurs a few days to weeks before death, in which the desire to eat and drink decreases, and the person may feel restless, irritable, and anxious. The second stage is the active stage, where the skin begins to cool, breathing becomes difficult as the lungs become congested (known as the "death rattle"), and the person loses control of their bodily fluids.

Once death occurs, there are also two stages. The first is clinical death, when the heart stops pumping blood and breathing ceases. This stage lasts approximately 4-6 minutes,

and during this time, it is possible for a victim to be resuscitated via CPR or a defibrillator. After 6 minutes however, the oxygen stores within the brain begin to deplete, and the victim enters biological death. This is the point of no return, as the cells of the brain and vital organs begin to die, a process that is irreversible.

Passage II

It was her sister Josephine who told her, in broken sentences; veiled hints that revealed in half concealing. Her husband's friend Richards was there, too, near her. It was he who had been in the newspaper office when intelligence of the railroad disaster was received, with Brently Mallard's name leading the list of "killed." He had only taken the time to assure himself of its truth by a second telegram, and had hastened to forestall any less careful, less tender friend in bearing the sad message.

She did not hear the story as many women have heard the same, with a paralyzed inability to accept its significance. She wept at once, with sudden, wild abandonment, in her sister's arms. When the storm of grief had spent itself she went away to her room alone. She would have no one follow her.

There stood, facing the open window, a comfortable, roomy armchair. Into this she sank, pressed down by a physical exhaustion that haunted her body and seemed to reach into her soul.

Excerpt from "The Story of an Hour" by Kate Chopin

Now, using the outline above, the similarities and differences between the two passages are considered:

1. **Style:** Passage I is an expository style, presenting purely factual evidence on death, completely devoid of emotion. Passage II is a narrative style, where the theme of death is presented to us by the reaction of the loved ones involved. This narrative style is full of emotional language and imagery.

2. **Tone:** Passage I has no emotionally-charged words of any kind, and seems to view death simply as a process that happens, neither welcoming nor fearing it. The tone in this passage, therefore, is neutral. Passage II does not have a neutral tone—it uses words like "disaster," "killed," "sad," "wept," "wild abandonment," and "physical exhaustion," implying an anxiety toward the theme of death.

3. **Sentence Structure:** Passage I contains many complex-compound sentences, which are used to accommodate lots of information. The structure of these sentences contributes to the overall informative nature of the selection. Passage II has several compound sentences and complex sentences on their own. It's also marked by the use of many commas in a single sentence, separating modifying words. Perhaps this variety is meant to match the sporadic emotion of the character's discovery of her husband's death.

4. **Punctuation Choice:** Passage I uses only commas and periods, which adds to the overall neutral tone of the selection. Passage II mostly uses commas and periods, and then one semicolon. Again, the excess of commas and semicolon in the first sentence may be said to mirror the character's anxiety.

5. Point of View: Passage I uses third-person point of view, as it avoids any first- or second-person pronouns. Passage II also uses third-person point of view, as the story is being told by a narrator about characters separate from the narrator.

6. Paragraph Structure: The first passage is told in an objective way, and each paragraph is focused on the topic brought up in the first sentence. The second passage has no specific topic per paragraph. It is organized in a sequential way, so the paragraphs flow into the next in a chronological order.

7. Organizational Structure: The structure of Passage I is told in a very objective, organized way. The first paragraph tells of the stages before death, and the second paragraph tells of the stages after death. The second passage is told in chronological order, as a sequence of events, like in a fictional story.

When analyzing the different structures, it may be helpful to make a table and use single words to compare and contrast the texts:

Elements	Passage I	Passage II
Style	Expository	Narrative
Tone	Neutral	Emotional
Sentence Structure	Long	Long/Sporadic
Punctuation Choice	.	. and ,
Point of View	Third	Third
Paragraph Structure	Focused	Sequential
Organizational Structure	Objective/Logical	Chronological

The main differences between the two selections are style, tone, and structure. Possibly the most noticeable difference is the style and tone, as one tone is more neutral, and the other tone is more emotional. This is due to the word choice used and how each passage treats the topic of death. These are only a handful of the endless possible interpretations the reader could make.

Constructing Arguments Through Evidence

Using only one form of supporting evidence is not nearly as effective as using a variety to support a claim. Presenting only a list of statistics can be boring to the reader but providing a true story that's both interesting and humanizing helps. In addition, one example isn't always enough to prove the writer's larger point, so combining it with other examples in the writing is extremely effective. Thus, when reading a passage, readers should not just look for a single form of supporting evidence.

For example, although most people can't argue with the statement, "Seat belts save lives," its impact on the reader is much greater when supported by additional content. The writer can support this idea by:

- Providing statistics on the rate of highway fatalities alongside statistics of estimated seat belt usage.

- Explaining the science behind car accidents and what happens to a passenger who doesn't use a seat belt.

- Offering anecdotal evidence or true stories from reliable sources on how seat belts prevent fatal injuries in car crashes.

Another key aspect of supporting evidence is a **reliable source**. Does the writer include the source of the information? If so, is the source well-known and trustworthy? Is there a potential for bias? For example, a seat belt study done by a seat belt manufacturer may have its own agenda to promote.

Logical Sequence

Even if the writer includes plenty of information to support his or her point, the writing is only effective when the information is in a logical order. **Logical sequencing** is really just common sense, but it's also an important writing technique. First, the writer should introduce the main idea, whether for a paragraph, a section, or the entire text. Then he or she should present evidence to support the main idea by using transitional language. This shows the reader how the information relates to the main idea and to the sentences around it. The writer should then take time to interpret the information, making sure necessary connections are obvious to the reader. Finally, the writer can summarize the information in the closing section.

NOTE: Although most writing follows this pattern, it isn't a set rule. Sometimes writers change the order for effect. For example, the writer can begin with a surprising piece of supporting information to grab the reader's attention, and then transition to the main idea. Thus, if a passage doesn't follow the logical order, readers should not immediately assume it's wrong. However, most writing that has a nontraditional beginning usually settles into a logical sequence.

Text Completion

General Information

The **Text Completion** section of the GRE assesses the reader's ability to comprehend a passage by filling in missing words from a paragraph. The correct word choice(s) will clarify the meaning of the ideas that were organized and developed by the author. A critical reading of a passage means that the reader can break down complex concepts into accessible units. By evaluating the relationships of the parts to the whole, the skilled reader can determine the best word option that gives meaning to a sentence.

Question Format

Readers will see one to three blank columns, which contain options for the fill-in-the blank word. Unless otherwise stated, three answer choices will be provided for each blank. To receive full credit for the question, readers should be sure to select one option for each blank.

Readers may fill in the blanks in any order. If the answer to one blank is apparent, a previous blank (or a later blank) might be easier to fill in.

Suggestions

Reading and Understanding the Passage

- Readers should evaluate the sequence of main and sub-points and transitions to decipher the author's intended meaning.

- Another way for readers to better understand the passage is to practice reading more slowly if they cannot identify logical patterns and transitions from one point to the next. If readers do not comprehend the meaning and the context of what the writer intended to communicate, they will be at a disadvantage when selecting the correct answers to the questions.

- Readers should infer the main point of a sentence based on the information provided.

- Readers should always be ready to support their answer with information that is provided in the sentence. Answer choices that are too extreme or too simplistic should be avoided.

Filling in the Blanks with One's Own Words

Readers should fill in the meaning of the passage with their own words, then see if there are similar words in the list. If readers cannot create a reasonable summary in their mind, they should reread the relevant points to gain more comprehensive knowledge of the passage.

Practice Example

Select the best word from the corresponding column of choices that most clearly completes the passage.

1. With the constant growth of (i) _____, higher education curriculum design and delivery systems are transforming to adapt to a new community of learners. Potential students may choose from a menu of traditional, blended, and online delivery systems. To keep up with mobile technology, students may also select to engage in mLearning—learning from mobile devices—and uLearning, or (ii) _____ learning, meaning learning that can happen anywhere, inside or outside of a classroom, with or without teachers, and with or without fellow learners. Significantly, the pedagogical concern is that the learning units remain curriculum-based to assure that learning objectives are created and met. As learning is unbundled from traditional delivery systems, it is important for curriculum designers to include models like Bloom's (iii) _____ of learning, the theory that learning begins as a repetition of facts and moves up the hierarchy to develop more complex critical thinking skills.

Blank (i)	Blank (ii)	Blank (iii)
a. Technology	d. Undulating	g. Taxonomy
b. Plagiarism	e. Ubiquitous	h. Anachronism
c. Resignations	f. Untenable	i. Panegyric

Explanation:

As one reads the passage for its broad meaning, it becomes obvious that a dominant theme of the piece focuses on learning in a higher education environment. As one considers the choices in the first blank, *plagiarism* (Choice *B*) and *resignation* (Choice *C*) both suggest a negative tone. The passage's sub-points, however, do not indicate a negative point of view. As one reads more about the introduction of mobile technology and higher education curriculum design, the term *uLearning* has a corresponding term that

begins with the letter "u." All the words in column (ii) begin with the letter "u," so readers must use a process of elimination. Because *ubiquitous* means existing everywhere at the same time, completing the sentence with the word *ubiquitous* completes the definition of *uLearning*. Finally, if readers are familiar with the learning models in education, they will remember that Bloom's taxonomy of learning makes the best possible choice for the final blank. Therefore, *technology* (Choice *A*) is the correct answer for the first blank, *ubiquitous* (Choice *E*) is the correct answer for the second blank, and *taxonomy* (Choice *G*) is the correct answer for the third and final blank.

Select the best word from the corresponding column of choices that most clearly completes the passage.

2. Queen Elizabeth I was known for her (i) _____ passion for overcoming challenges; however, her competitors wished she was more (ii) _____ in governing.

Blank (i)	Blank (ii)
a. Wretched	d. Voracious
b. Pusillanimous	e. Obdurate
c. Sedulous	f. Tractable

Explanation:

Breaking down the larger concepts of overcoming challenges and competition, readers can quickly recognize that a word like *sedulous*—which means diligent, persevering, or persistent—is the best choice for the first blank. *Pusillanimous* means timid, which does not fit the theme of overcoming challenges, and *wretched* suggests pity or misfortune, which does not complement the notion of beating the odds. For the second blank, a word that denotes a characteristic that would be pleasing for Queen Elizabeth's competitors in governing should be considered. Therefore, *tractable* is the best choice for the sentence because it means she could be easily persuaded. The correct answer for blank (i) is *sedulous* (Choice *C*), and the correct answer for blank (ii) is *tractable* (Choice *F*).

Sentence Equivalence

General Information

The GRE **Sentence Equivalence** section tests a reader's ability to complete the full meaning of a sentence by supplying two of six possible word choices. Unlike traditional fill-in-the-blank tests, sentence equivalence questions ask for two words that are similar in meaning and that complete the meaning of the sentence. One note of caution: the meaning of the two words should be similar, but they do not necessarily have to be synonyms to be correct.

Checking for Logic, Grammar, and Style

Similar to the Text Completion section, readers should check the logic and grammar to determine which two best answer options fit the blank. To create a coherent sentence, each word should be tried in the blank to see which ones lend rational meaning to the sentence. The two words should relate to each other, and they also must each separately fit into the sentence's context in a logical manner.

It may also help for readers to be aware that the two correct answer choices will have grammatically similar parts of speech. Usually the answer options will be made up of nouns, verbs, and adjectives. Again, test takers should pay attention to the context of the sentence to see which words precede or

follow the blank in order to determine which answer options to rule out. Words should be chosen that fit within the blank stylistically as well.

Question Format

- The sentence will have one missing word indicated by a blank space.
- Readers will choose two similar words from a list of six options that best complete the sentence.
- Readers should make sure the two words not only share similar meanings, but that they also correctly complete the meaning of the sentence.

Suggestions

Reading and Understanding the Passage

Readers must be sure to develop a comprehensive, high-level vocabulary as a pretest strategy. Reading high-level material is the best way to come across relevant vocabulary in context. Also, readers should keep a running word list complete with definitions and synonym/antonym relationships. Looking for synonyms is one strategy for identifying correct choices on the Sentence Equivalence section of the test.

Readers should keep in mind during GRE study time that general and daily reading is essential if one intends to do well on the Verbal Reasoning section of the test. Readers can keep a list of GRE frequently used words and their definitions and practice memorizing these words for future use. Using flashcards is another way that one can speed up the learning experience.

Filling in the Blanks with One's Own Words

Readers should try to fill in the blank with their own word first. If a reader starts filling in the blank with the word choices supplied below the sentence, he or she may go off on the wrong track regarding the true meaning the writer intended. After a fill-in word is chosen, readers may look for similarities in the answer options. Remember that even though the words may not be synonyms, they should have similar meanings.

If readers know the definitions of all the answer options, another strategy is to plug sets of words into the blank in the sentence. If the selected words complete the overall meaning of the sentence, they are probably correct.

Practice Examples

Select two words that are similar in meaning to complete the sentence correctly and sensibly.

1. The lawyer, who began his presentation in a (an) _____ manner, faltered when new evidence was presented.
    a. Cogent
    b. Persuasive
    c. Ineffective
    d. Verbose
    e. Vacuous
    f. Phlegmatic

Explanation:

At first glance, several of the words could complete the sentence about the manner in which the lawyer presented his case. However, readers should select two words that are not only similar in meaning, but that also make the most sense in the context of the sentence. Readers will note that *ineffective* does not have a partner word. Yes, *verbose* makes sense, but it does not have a word of similar meaning, and *vacuous* and *phlegmatic* do not complete the sentence in a sensible way. Therefore, the correct pair is *cogent* and *persuasive*. They both mean "compelling," and they could be used interchangeably in the sentence.

The correct responses are Choice *A* (*cogent*), and Choice *B* (*persuasive*).

Select two words that are similar in meaning to complete the sentence correctly and sensibly.

2. If there is a remote possibility of winning the championship game, the players must practice without _____.

    a. Apathy
    b. Ardor
    c. Fervor
    d. Ennui
    e. Vigor
    f. Zeal

Explanation:

If readers understand the meaning of all the words, the best two words to complete the sentence stand out. Because players will need to increase their energy and power during practice, readers should select two words that suggest opposite ideas. It may be obvious that *zeal*, *fervor*, and *vigor* all share similar ideas. If readers are not sure what *ennui* means, they can make an educated guess that apathy and ardor are not synonyms. Therefore, the best words are *ennui* and *apathy* because they both suggest playing with a sense of boredom and detachment.

The correct responses are Choice *A* (*apathy*) and Choice *D* (*ennui*)

GRE Verbal Practice Test #1

Text Completion

Select the best word from the corresponding column of choices that most clearly completes the passage:

1. At one time, the Roman Empire was one of the most (i) _____ military, economic, political, and cultural forces in the world. Around 100 BC, Rome was one of the largest and most (ii) _____ cities in the world. It was an influential (iii) _____ of the modern world.

Blank (i)	Blank (ii)	Blank (iii)
a. Acerbic	d. Potent	g. Acumen
b. Perspicacious	e. Obscure	h. Convention
c. Robust	f. Obsolete	i. Precursor

2. The term *introvert* was made popular by the theories of Carl Jung. An introverted personality displays (i) _____ personality traits. Usually, an introvert will not be the first volunteer to host a (ii) _____ event.

Blank (i)	Blank (ii)
a. Loquacious	d. Grandiose
b. Taciturn	e. Decorous
c. Verbose	f. Punctilious

3. The (i) _____ outer covering of the tadpole prevented the biologist from determining the stage of development of the internal organs.

Blank (i)
a. Luminous
b. Opaque
c. Sheer
d. Clear
e. Scaly

4. The members' (i) _____ conversations gave way to one praiseworthy speech that (ii) _____ the reputation of the new president.

Blank (i)	Blank (ii)
a. Garrulous	d. Lauded
b. Reserved	e. Diminished
c. Inhibited	f. Occluded

5. The chemist was disappointed when the solid structures began to (i) _____, making his scientific expected outcome the opposite of what he had hoped.

Blank (i)
a. Petrify
b. Congeal
c. Stiffen
d. Liquefy
e. Fossilize

6. The search for the great (i) _____ made all other adventures seem (ii) _____ for the seasoned sailors.

Blank (i)	Blank (ii)
a. Achillobator	d. Pedestrian
b. Titanis	e. Erudite
c. Leviathan	f. Imperious

7. Much to the delight of the defense attorney, the detectives were able to (i) _____ that the prisoner on death row was actually innocent, by using DNA testing.

Blank (i)
a. Occlude
b. Infer
c. Prevaricate
d. Deny
e. Celebrate

8. The famous paintings of Caspar David Friedrich, appreciated by patrons of Expressionism, do not convey the same (i) _____ emotion as the more (ii) _____ landscapes of the earlier Expressionist masters.

Blank (i)	Blank (ii)
a. Aesthetic	d. Classical
b. Maudlin	e. Spiritual
c. Effusive	f. Abstract

9. The obvious (i) _____ of the conquerors made the humiliated tribe dubious about promises of fair or humane treatment in the future.

Blank (i)
a. Depredation
b. Retrieval
c. Convalescence
d. Boon
e. Restoration

10. The renowned Pharaoh Ahmose I, who was not (i) _____by the complexity of a construction plan, was remembered for his ability to cultivate an (ii) _____ building plan. Ahmose I oversaw the construction of the last native-built Egyptian pyramid.

Blank (i)	Blank (ii)
a. Inhibited	d. Ingenious
b. Mitigated	e. Indigenous
c. Placated	f. Insular

11. The representatives of the administration selected new interns, hoping that the important and applicable principles taught to them in college had a chance to (i) _____over the summer.

Blank (i)
a. Soften
b. Ossify
c. Dissipate
d. Multiply
e. Disintegrate

12. The frightened coyote, trying to escape from the (i) _____ cougar, shifted his weight in the nick of time to avoid the edge of the (ii) _____, and the (iii) _____ intentions of the approaching cougar.

Blank (i)	Blank (ii)	Blank (iii)
a. Irascible	d. Precipice	g. Ponderous
b. Magnanimous	e. Buttress	h. Malevolent
c. Phlegmatic	f. Encomium	i. Sanguine

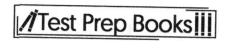

13. Even after eating three full meals and several snacks, the athlete was not (i) _____ to his appetite's satisfaction.

Blank (i)
a. Sated
b. Deprived
c. Lavished
d. Recompensed
e. Immured

14. Alison Creek, a waterway located in California that winds from the mountains to the Pacific Ocean, could not be used as a viable source of drinking water because of its unpredictable and (i) _____ quality. The concerns of the municipality were (ii) _____ by the suggested alternate use of the coastal area for recreational purposes.

Blank (i)	Blank (ii)
a. Erratic	d. Intensified
b. Invariable	e. Assuaged
c. Consistent	f. Exacerbated

15. In the fifth century BC, Herodotus shared his interpretations of culture and politics as a great historian and scholar. Even though his stories may have (i) _____ reality, as he added excessive details, he was often referred to as "the father of history."

Blank (i)
a. Propitiated
b. Precipitated
c. Exacerbated
d. Aggrandized
e. Emulated

16. In the (i) _____ field of big data, a recent term used to identify very large collections of data and statistical analysis, many scholarly researchers are contributing significant findings to Fortune 500 research and development programs.

Blank (i)
a. Diminishing
b. Burgeoning
c. Ambiguous
d. Disparaging
e. Floundering

Reading Comprehension

Questions 17–20 are based on the following passage:

The town of Alexandria, Virginia was founded in 1749. Between the years 1810 and 1861, this thriving seaport was the ideal location for slave owners such as Joseph Bruin, Henry Hill, Isaac Franklin, and John Armfield to build several slave trade office structures, including slave holding areas. After 1830, when the manufacturing-based economy slowed down in Virginia, slaves were traded to plantations in the Deep South, in Alabama, Mississippi, and Louisiana. Joseph Bruin, one of the most notorious of the slave traders operating in Alexandria, alone purchased hundreds of slaves from 1844 to 1861. Harriet Beecher Stowe claimed that the horrible slave traders mentioned in her novel, *Uncle Tom's Cabin*, are reminiscent of the coldhearted Joseph Bruin. The Franklin and Armfield Office was known as one of the largest slave trading companies in the country up to the end of the Civil War period. Slaves, waiting to be traded, were held in a two-story slave pen built behind the Franklin and Armfield Office structure on Duke Street in Alexandria. Yet, many people fought to thwart these traders and did everything they could to rescue and free slaves. Two Christian African American slave sisters, with the help of northern abolitionists who bought their freedom, escaped Bruin's plan to sell them into southern prostitution. In 1861, Joseph Bruin was captured and imprisoned and his property confiscated. The Bruin Slave Jail became the Fairfax County courthouse until 1865. The original Franklin and Armfield Office building still stands in Virginia and is registered in the National Register of Historic Places. The Bruin Slave Jail is still standing on Duke Street in Alexandria, but is not open to the public. The history of the slave trading enterprise is preserved and presented to the public by the Northern Virginia Urban League.

Consider each of the choices separately and select all that apply:

17. Based on the above passage, which of the following statements about the town of Alexandria are true?

a. Alexandria was a seaport town, which could not prosper, even with the advent of a slave trade business, because the manufacturing industry was not enough to stabilize the economy.

b. Slave traders such as Joseph Bruin, Henry Hill, Isaac Franklin, and John Armfield rented both slave trade office buildings and slave holding buildings from landlords of Old Town, Alexandria.

c. For over fifteen years, Joseph Bruin, a notorious slave trader, probably the one characterized in *Uncle Tom's Cabin*, bought hundreds of slaves with the intention of sending the purchased slaves to southern states such as Alabama, Mississippi, and Louisiana.

d. The Bruin Slave Jail is open to the public; the building is located in downtown Alexandria, and still stands in Virginia. The jail is registered in the National Register of Historic Places. The history of the slave trading enterprise is preserved and presented to the public by the Northern Virginia Urban League.

e. Isaac Franklin and John Armfield's slave-trade office structures, including slave holding areas in downtown Alexandria, remained open for their slave trade business until the end of the Civil War.

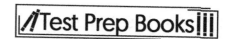

Consider each of the choices separately and select all that apply:

18. The passage about the Alexandria slave trade business suggests that which of the following statements can be regarded as true?

a. The lucrative seaport town of Alexandria was supported by successful slave trade businesses of men like Joseph Bruin, Henry Hill, Isaac Franklin, and John Armfield, who bought slaves and sold them to the plantations in the Deep South.

b. Joseph Bruin, a highly respected Alexandrian businessman, ran a slave trade business in downtown Alexandria, until the business closed its doors at the end of the Civil War.

c. The Franklin and Armfield Office was built by Isaac Franklin and John Armfield. Slaves, waiting to be traded, were held in a four-story slave pen built behind the Franklin and Armfield Office structure on Duke Street in Alexandria.

d. When the Confederate Army positioned its command in Alexandria, and closed slave traders' businesses, the Franklin and Armfield slave pen became the Fairfax County courthouse and was used to hold Union soldiers.

e. The literature of the slave trading enterprise, like *Uncle Tom's Cabin*, is being preserved and presented to the public by the Northern Virginia Urban League.

Consider each of the choices separately and select all that apply:

19. Which of the following statements can be inferred to be accurate, based on the information provided in the passage?

a. The town of Alexandria, founded in 1810, became one of the most infamous slave trading markets in the country.

b. Harriet Beecher Stowe was an escaped slave who was held in the Franklin and Armfield slave pen, located on Duke Street in Alexandria. To avoid a life as a prostitute, Miss Stowe tried to escape from the control of Joseph Bruin, whose surly characteristics surfaced in her classic book, *Uncle Tom's Cabin*.

c. Northern abolitionists were known to help runaway slaves escape the hands of their notorious owners.

d. The Bruin Slave Jail, located in downtown Alexandria, still stands today, although it is not open for public viewing.

e. For convenience, the slave traders took their slaves to nearby Annapolis, Maryland, because the cost of shipping them from there was less than the cost of shipping them from Alexandria.

Select only one answer choice:

20. Which of the following statements best illustrates the author's intended main point or thesis?

a. Two Christian African American slave sisters, with the help of northern abolitionists who bought their freedom, escaped Bruin's plan to sell them into southern prostitution.

b. The town of Alexandria, a thriving seaport founded in 1749, was the location for several lucrative slave trading companies from 1810 to 1861.

c. After the start of the Civil War, Joseph Bruin was captured and his jail was no longer used for his slave trade business.

d. The Bruin Slave Jail is still standing on Duke Street in Alexandria, but is not open to the public.

e. In 1861, the Bruin Slave Jail in Alexandria became the Fairfax County courthouse.

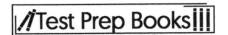

Questions 21–25 are based upon the following passage:

My Good Friends,—When I first imparted to the committee of the projected Institute my particular wish that on one of the evenings of my readings here the main body of my audience should be composed of working men and their families, I was animated by two desires; first, by the wish to have the great pleasure of meeting you face to face at this Christmas time, and accompany you myself through one of my little Christmas books; and second, by the wish to have an opportunity of stating publicly in your presence, and in the presence of the committee, my earnest hope that the Institute will, from the beginning, recognise one great principle—strong in reason and justice—which I believe to be essential to the very life of such an Institution. It is, that the working man shall, from the first unto the last, have a share in the management of an Institution which is designed for his benefit, and which calls itself by his name.

I have no fear here of being misunderstood—of being supposed to mean too much in this. If there ever was a time when any one class could of itself do much for its own good, and for the welfare of society—which I greatly doubt—that time is unquestionably past. It is in the fusion of different classes, without confusion; in the bringing together of employers and employed; in the creating of a better common understanding among those whose interests are identical, who depend upon each other, who are vitally essential to each other, and who never can be in unnatural antagonism without deplorable results, that one of the chief principles of a Mechanics' Institution should consist. In this world, a great deal of the bitterness among us arises from an imperfect understanding of one another. Erect in Birmingham a great Educational Institution, properly educational; educational of the feelings as well as of the reason; to which all orders of Birmingham men contribute; in which all orders of Birmingham men meet; wherein all orders of Birmingham men are faithfully represented—and you will erect a Temple of Concord here which will be a model edifice to the whole of England.

Contemplating as I do the existence of the Artisans' Committee, which not long ago considered the establishment of the Institute so sensibly, and supported it so heartily, I earnestly entreat the gentlemen—earnest I know in the good work, and who are now among us—by all means to avoid the great shortcoming of similar institutions; and in asking the working man for his confidence, to set him the great example and give him theirs in return. You will judge for yourselves if I promise too much for the working man, when I say that he will stand by such an enterprise with the utmost of his patience, his perseverance, sense, and support; that I am sure he will need no charitable aid or condescending patronage; but will readily and cheerfully pay for the advantages which it confers; that he will prepare himself in individual cases where he feels that the adverse circumstances around him have rendered it necessary; in a word, that he will feel his responsibility like an honest man, and will most honestly and manfully discharge it. I now proceed to the pleasant task to which I assure you I have looked forward for a long time.

From Charles Dickens' speech in Birmingham in England on December 30, 1853 on behalf of the Birmingham and Midland Institute.

Select only one answer choice:

21. The speaker addresses his audience as *My Good Friends*. What kind of credibility does this salutation give to the speaker?

    a. The speaker is an employer addressing his employees, so the salutation is a way for the boss to bridge the gap between himself and his employees.

    b. The speaker's salutation is one from an entertainer to his audience and uses the friendly language to connect to his audience before a serious speech.

    c. The salutation is used ironically to give a somber tone to the serious speech that follows.

    d. The speech is one from a politician to the public, so the salutation is used to grab the audience's attention.

Select only one answer choice:

22. According to the passage, what is the speaker's second desire for his time in front of the audience?

    a. To read a Christmas story

    b. For the working man to have a say in his institution, which is designed for his benefit

    c. To have an opportunity to stand in their presence

    d. For the life of the institution to be essential to the audience as a whole

Select only one answer choice:

23. The speaker's tone in the passage can be described as:

    a. Happy and gullible

    b. Lazy and entitled

    c. Confident and informed

    d. Angry and frustrated

Select only one answer choice:

24. One of the main purposes of the last paragraph is:

    a. To persuade the audience to support the Institute no matter what since it provided so much support to the working class.

    b. To market the speaker's new book while at the same time supporting the activities of the Institute.

    c. To inform the audience that the Institute is corrupt and will not help them out when the time comes to give them compensation.

    d. To provide credibility to the working man and share confidence in their ability to take on responsibilities if they are compensated appropriately.

Select only one answer choice:

25. According to the passage, what does the speaker wish to erect in Birmingham?

    a. An Educational Institution

    b. The Temple of Concord

    c. A Writing Workshop

    d. A VA Hospital

Questions 26–30 are based on the following passage:

Learning how to write a ten-minute play may seem like a monumental task at first; but, if you follow a simple creative writing strategy, similar to writing a narrative story, you will be able to write a successful drama. The first step is to open your story as if it is a puzzle to be solved. This will allow the reader a moment to engage with the story and to mentally solve the story with you, the author. Immediately provide descriptive details that steer the main idea, the tone, and the mood according to the overarching theme you have in mind. For example, if the play is about something ominous, you may open Scene One with a thunderclap. Next, use dialogue to reveal the attitudes and personalities of each of the characters who have a key part in the unfolding story. Keep the characters off balance in some way to create interest and dramatic effect. Maybe what the characters say does not match what they do. Show images on stage to speed up the narrative; remember, one picture speaks a thousand words. As the play progresses, the protagonist must cross the point of no return in some way; this is the climax of the story. Then, as in a written story, you create a resolution to the life-changing event of the protagonist. Let the characters experience some kind of self-discovery that can be understood and appreciated by the patient audience. Finally, make sure all things come together in the end so that every detail in the play makes sense right before the curtain falls.

Select only one answer choice:

26. Based on the passage above, which of the following statements is FALSE?
    a. Writing a ten-minute play may seem like an insurmountable task.
    b. Providing descriptive details is not necessary until after the climax of the story line.
    c. Engaging the audience by jumping into the story line immediately helps the audience solve the story's developing ideas with you, the writer.
    d. Descriptive details give clues to the play's intended mood and tone.
    e. The introduction of a ten-minute play does not need to open with a lot of coffee pouring or cigarette smoking to introduce the scenes. The action can get started right away.

Select only one answer choice:

27. Based on the passage above, which of the following is true?
    a. The class of eighth graders quickly learned that it is not that difficult to write a ten-minute play.
    b. The playwrights of the twenty-first century all use the narrative writing basic feature guide to outline their initial scripts.
    c. In order to follow a simple structure, a person can write a ten-minute play based on some narrative writing features.
    d. Women find playwriting easier than men because they are used to communicating in writing.
    e. The structure of writing a poem is similar to that of play writing and of narrative writing.

Consider each of the choices separately and select all that apply:

28. Based on your understanding of the passage, it can be assumed that which of the following statements are true?
    a. One way to reveal the identities and nuances of the characters in a play is to use dialogue.
    b. Characters should follow predictable routes in the challenge presented in the unfolding narrative, so the audience may easily follow the sequence of events.
    c. Using images in the stage design is an important element of creating atmosphere and meaning for the drama.
    d. There is no need for the protagonist to come to terms with a self-discovery; he or she simply needs to follow the prescription for life lived as usual.
    e. It is perfectly fine to avoid serious consequences for the actors of a ten-minute play because there is not enough time to unravel perils.

Select only one answer choice:

29. In the passage, the writer suggests that writing a ten-minute play is accessible for a novice playwright because of which of the following reasons?
    a. It took the author of the passage only one week to write his first play.
    b. The format follows similar strategies of writing a narrative story.
    c. There are no particular themes or points to unravel; a playwright can use a stream of consciousness style to write a play.
    d. Dialogue that reveals the characters' particularities is uncommonly simple to write.
    e. The characters of a ten-minute play wrap up the action simply by revealing their ideas in a monologue.

Select only one answer choice:

30. Based on the passage, which basic feature of narrative writing is NOT mentioned with respect to writing a ten-minute play?
    a. Character development
    b. Descriptive details
    c. Dialogue
    d. Mood and tone
    e. Style

Questions 31–34 are based on the following passage:

An Organization for Economic Cooperation and Development study of ten developing countries during the period from 1985 to 1992 found significant implementation of privatization in only three countries. The study concluded that "reductions in the central budget deficit can only be marginal" because the impact was not evaluated over several years to consider the effect of the revenues foregone from state-owned enterprises (SOEs). Several later studies measured the budgetary effects and reported significant increases in profitability and productivity as a result of privatization, but the methodological flaws related to the difficulty of isolating the performance of SOEs from other elements rendered the findings ambiguous. While the evidence on the performance of SOEs "shows that state ownership is often correlated with politicization, inefficiency, and waste of resources," the assumption that it is state ownership that creates an environment influencing the quality of performance is not proven, with the empirical research on this point having yielded conflicting results. Given the inconclusive evidence, many scholars

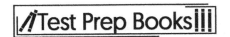

did not concur on a World Bank statement in 1995 that SOEs "remain an important obstacle to better economic performance."

Reflecting a belief that the market is the best allocator of resources, experts have often recommended "unleashing" the private sector by removing regulations and privatizing SOEs. In 1995, to preclude hasty and simplistic privatization efforts, the World Bank recommended that SOEs be corporatized under commercial law and issued guidance on "[p]re-privatization interim measures and institutional arrangements for 'permanent SOEs.'" The bank also listed five preconditions for successful privatization: hard budget constraints; capital and labor market discipline; competition; corporate governance free of political interference; and commitment to privatization.

In view of the pervasive presence of SOEs in the global economy and their embodiment of political and economic considerations, SOEs are an entity to be considered and managed in the pursuit of stability.

"The State-Owned Enterprise as a Vehicle for Stability" by Neil Efird (2010), published by the Strategic Studies Institute (Department of Defense), pgs. 7–8

Consider each of the choices separately and select all that apply:

31. The World Bank issued which statement(s) in 1995?
    a. State-owned enterprises can impede economic performance.
    b. State-owned enterprises play a critical role in developing countries.
    c. State-owned enterprises promote economic and political stability.
    d. State-owned enterprises should be corporatized under commercial law gradually.
    e. State-owned enterprises might be inefficient, but the evidence is inconclusive.

Select only one answer choice:

32. Based on the passage above, which statement(s) can be properly inferred?
    a. State-owned enterprises always cause economic stagnation.
    b. Privatization is controversial, even among economic experts.
    c. Economic studies are always subject to intense criticism and secondhand guessing.
    d. State-owned enterprises violate commercial law.
    e. The World Bank holds the power to directly intervene in economies.

Consider each of the choices separately and select all that apply:

33. Which statement(s) about state-owned enterprises is true based on the passage above?
    a. The empirical research demonstrates that state-owned enterprises are efficient and productive.
    b. Developing countries have little influence on the World Bank's policies.
    c. Privatization enjoys widespread popular support wherever it is implemented.
    d. State-owned enterprises have sizable effects on the global economy.
    e. Among other factors, successful privatization requires competition and corporate governance that is free of political interference.

Select only one answer choice:

34. Which statement(s) most accurately identifies the author's ultimate conclusion?
    a. The market is the best allocator of resources, so private enterprises will always outperform state-owned enterprises.
    b. The World Bank holds considerable expertise in matters related to state-owned enterprises and privatization.
    c. State-owned enterprises should be managed in a way that promotes economic stability, which might require a measured approach to privatization.
    d. Studies conducted with a flawed methodology should not be the basis for economic decisions.
    e. State-owned enterprises should be privatized under commercial law as long as the government adheres to the five preconditions for privatization.

Questions 35–41 are based on the following passages.

Passage I

Lethal force, or deadly force, is defined as the physical means to cause death or serious harm to another individual. The law holds that lethal force is only accepted when you or another person are in immediate and unavoidable danger of death or severe bodily harm. For example, a person could be beating a weaker person in such a way that they are suffering severe enough trauma that could result in death or serious harm. This would be an instance where lethal force would be acceptable and possibly the only way to save that person from irrevocable damage.

Another example of when to use lethal force would be when someone enters your home with a deadly weapon. The intruder's presence and possession of the weapon indicate mal-intent and the ability to inflict death or severe injury to you and your loved ones. Again, lethal force can be used in this situation. Lethal force can also be applied to prevent the harm of another individual. If a woman is being brutally assaulted and is unable to fend off an attacker, lethal force can be used to defend her as a last-ditch effort. If she is in immediate jeopardy of rape, harm, and/or death, lethal force could be the only response that could effectively deter the assailant.

The key to understanding the concept of lethal force is the term *last resort*. Deadly force cannot be taken back; it should be used only to prevent severe harm or death. The law does distinguish whether the means of one's self-defense is fully warranted, or if the individual goes out of control in the process. If you continually attack the assailant after they are rendered incapacitated, this would be causing unnecessary harm, and the law can bring charges against you. Likewise, if you kill an attacker unnecessarily after defending yourself, you can be charged with murder. This would move lethal force beyond necessary defense, making it no longer a last resort but rather a use of excessive force.

Passage II

Assault is the unlawful attempt of one person to apply apprehension on another individual by an imminent threat or by initiating offensive contact. Assaults can vary, encompassing physical strikes, threatening body language, and even provocative language. In the case of the latter, even if a hand has not been laid, it is still considered an assault because of its threatening nature.

Let's look at an example: A homeowner is angered because his neighbor blows fallen leaves into his freshly mowed lawn. Irate, the homeowner gestures a fist to his fellow neighbor and threatens to bash his head in for littering on his lawn. The homeowner's physical motions and verbal threat heralds a physical threat against the other neighbor. These factors classify the homeowner's reaction as an assault. If the angry neighbor hits the threatening homeowner in retaliation, that would constitute an assault as well because he physically hit the homeowner.

Assault also centers on the involvement of weapons in a conflict. If someone fires a gun at another person, it could be interpreted as an assault unless the shooter acted in self-defense. If an individual drew a gun or a knife on someone with the intent to harm them, it would be considered assault. However, it's also considered an assault if someone simply aimed a weapon, loaded or not, at another person in a threatening manner.

Select only one answer choice:

35. What is the purpose of the second passage?
    a. To inform the reader about what assault is and how it is committed
    b. To inform the reader about how assault is a minor example of lethal force
    c. To disprove the previous passage concerning lethal force
    d. To argue that the use of assault is more common than the use of lethal force
    e. To recount an incident in which the author was assaulted

Select only one answer choice:

36. Which of the following situations, according to the passages, would not constitute an illegal use of lethal force?
    a. A disgruntled cashier yells obscenities at a customer.
    b. A thief is seen running away with stolen cash.
    c. A man is attacked in an alley by another man with a knife.
    d. A woman punches another woman in a bar.
    e. A driver accidently slams into another person's car and injures them.

Select only one answer choice:

37. Given the information in the passages, which of the following must be true about assault?
    a. All assault is considered an expression of lethal force.
    b. There are various forms of assault.
    c. Smaller, weaker people cannot commit assault.
    d. Assault is justified only as a last resort.
    e. Assault charges are more severe than unnecessary use of force charges.

Select only one answer choice:

38. Which of the following, if true, would most seriously undermine the explanation proposed by the author in the third paragraph of Passage I?
    a. An instance of lethal force in self-defense is not absolutely absolved from blame. The law takes into account the necessary use of force at the time it is committed.
    b. An individual who uses necessary defense under lethal force is in direct compliance of the law under most circumstances.
    c. Lethal force in self-defense should be forgiven in all cases for the peace of mind of the primary victim.
    d. The use of lethal force is not evaluated on the intent of the user but rather the severity of the primary attack that warranted self-defense.
    e. It's important to note that once lethal force goes beyond the necessary attempt to protect oneself, there's a chance it could turn into a deadly assault of excessive force.

Select only one answer choice:

39. Based on the passages, what can we infer about the relationship between assault and lethal force?
    a. An act of lethal force always leads to a type of assault.
    b. An assault will result in someone using lethal force.
    c. An assault with deadly intent can lead to an individual using lethal force to preserve their well-being.
    d. If someone uses self-defense in a conflict, it is called deadly force; if actions or threats are intended, it is called assault.
    e. Assault and lethal force have no conceivable connection.

Select only one answer choice:

40. Which of the following best describes the way the passages are structured?
    a. Both passages open by defining a legal concept and then continue to describe situations in order to further explain the concept.
    b. Both passages begin with situations, introduce accepted definitions, and then cite legal ramifications.
    c. The first passage presents a long definition while the second passage begins by showing an example of assault.
    d. Both cite specific legal doctrines, then proceed to explain the rulings.
    e. The first passage explains both concepts and then focuses on lethal force. The second passage picks up with assault and explains the concept in depth.

Select only one answer choice:

41. What can we infer about the role of intent in lethal force and assault?
    a. Intent is irrelevant. The law does not take intent into account.
    b. Intent is vital for determining the lawfulness of using lethal force.
    c. Intent is only taken into account for assault charges.
    d. The intent of the assailant is the main focus for determining legal ramifications; it is used to determine if the defender was justified in using force to respond.
    e. Intent is very important for determining both lethal force and assault; intent is examined in both parties and helps determine the severity of the issue.

Sentence Equivalence

Select the two answer choices that can complete the sentence and create sentences that have complementary meaning.

42. Obviously, the new hires were motivated at the beginning of the day, but after a full week of training and evaluations, they acted _____ when asked to perform one more test.
    a. Lackadaisical
    b. Indefatigable
    c. Lethargic
    d. Energized
    e. Vigorous
    f. Enterprising

43. Normally, I enjoy hearing new music that has an edgy sound; however, the music tonight sounded like a _____ of tones and beats that made me want to cover my ears.
    a. Accord
    b. Harmony
    c. Concordance
    d. Cacophony
    e. Composition
    f. Dissonance

44. The thief _____ with the purse before the geriatric patient knew someone was in the room.
    a. Yielded
    b. Absconded
    c. Appeared
    d. Erupted
    e. Bolted

45. The teacher recognized the immature writing style of the freshman because his essays used _____ language.
    a. Astute
    b. Apt
    c. Banal
    d. Trite
    e. Mediocre
    f. Middling

46. Unlike journalists, who avoid unsubstantiated narratives, politicians have a habit of _____ issues they find dubious.
    a. Pontificating
    b. Obscuring
    c. Explicating
    d. Obfuscating
    e. Discussing
    f. Confabulating

47. The model was asked to _____ the demands of her coach to eat salad and protein twice a day, because walking down the runway gave her such pleasure.
   a. Dissent to
   b. Accede to
   c. Disparage
   d. Acquiesce to
   e. Object to
   f. Castigate

48. Much to the _____ of the unprepared students, the new professor called on students randomly to deliver impromptu speeches to the class.
   a. Feint
   b. Chagrin
   c. Mortification
   d. Diatribe
   e. Enmity
   f. Exuberance

49. The debate team was poised and ready for a persuasive topic to be announced; they were hoping for opponents who were _____.
   a. Vacuous
   b. Fervid
   c. Flamboyant
   d. Fatuous
   e. Heinous
   f. Ineluctable

50. The two friends who attended the party quietly slipped downstairs where they could watch sports and avoid the _____ holiday movies that the couples insisted on watching.
   a. Maudlin
   b. Requisite
   c. Valorous
   d. Moribund
   e. Nefarious
   f. Quixotic

Answer Explanations #1

Text Completion

1. C, D, I: If the Roman military was robust and potent, then it would have been influential economically and culturally, which could have been a logical precursor to the developing modern world. Thus, *robust*, *potent*, and *precursor* are the three choices that would fit best within the sentence.

2. B, D: Introverted individuals are quieter than the more outspoken extroverts in a group. Knowing the characteristics of an introvert will help one select the correct answers. Both *verbose* and *loquacious* have to do with excessive speech, so *taciturn* is the answer for the first blank. *Grandiose* is the correct choice for the second blank, as an introvert does not like large, over-the-top events.

3. B: The key word in the sentence to signal an appropriate answer is "prevented." Therefore, the best answer cannot be *clear*, *sheer*, or *luminous*. The word *scaly* refers to the texture of the skin.

4. A, D: Readers should notice that the "praiseworthy speech" the members were giving sets the tone for their actions before and after. This will help one discern that a positive word, such as *lauded*, is necessary for the second blank. Therefore, the word *garrulous*, which means "excessive talking," would work for the intended meaning of the sentence with more clarity than either *reserved* or *inhibited*.

5. D: Many of the choices work grammatically with this sentence; however, the best option is the opposite of "solid" because that is the result that was unexpected in the scientist's mind. Therefore, the best possible answer based on the intended meaning of the sentence is *liquefy*.

6. C, D: Because the writer used *sailors*, the first blank must connect with a maritime adventure. Therefore, *leviathan* is the best choice for the first blank. A word that contrasts with an adventure is the word *pedestrian*, which signifies a more commonplace event.

7. B: In this case, the detectives are guessing or inferring that the original evidence was incorrect. *Deny* would not be the best answer because the defense attorney would not be happy if his client was found guilty. *Occlude* means to obstruct, which lacks reason when placed within the sentence; *prevaricate* means to act evasively, which is another logical problem when placed in the blank, as the detectives wouldn't "act evasively that the prisoner on death row was actually innocent." Although the defense attorney expresses delight, the option *celebrate* contradicts the mood of the passage.

8. A, D: If one is filling in the blanks individually, he or she may think of the term *aesthetic* because it captures the theme of the sentence. Similarly, the term *classical* is often used with master artists. In addition, the word *landscapes* helps to eliminate *spiritual* and *abstract* because they do not complete the idea of landscapes as well as the term *classical* does in this sentence.

9. A: There are several clues within the sentence to help readers select the choice with the best meaning that completes the sentence. For example, the word *humiliated* suggests that the conquerors were not only winning against the tribe, but that they also degraded them in the process. A *boon* is something that is good or an advantage for the recipient. Because an act of humiliation is not connected with the words *retrieval* or *convalescence*, the best choice is *depredation*.

10. A, D: The words *ability* and *cultivate* denote a certain confidence and forward-looking demeanor, thus, not being *inhibited* by a challenge makes the most sense. Challenges don't *placate* people; they often create anxiety. That Pharaoh Ahmose "oversaw" so much of the work also lets the reader know he was active and focused, so *ingenious* is the most logical choice. To be so involved would not make his ideas insular. *Indigenous* is more about staying with traditions or origins.

11. B: The representatives hoped that the principles the interns learned took hold or *ossified* over the summer break. The representatives wouldn't hope for the interns' principles to *soften, dissipate,* or *disintegrate.* The word *multiply* contradicts the logistics of the sentence, as pre-existing principles are incapable of *multiplying.*

12. A, D, H: The adverse words *irascible* and *malevolent* fit the first and last blanks best because the context implies an anxious, fearful atmosphere. The word *precipice* would fit best in the middle of the sentence because *buttresses* and *encomiums* don't have "edges" for coyotes to walk around on.

13. A: There is a clue to the answer of this question in the word "satisfaction." The root is similar to the choice, *sated*, which means "full to the brim." Some of the other choices are grammatically correct; however, they are not the best option to complete the meaning of the sentence.

14. A, E: If the water quality is "unpredictable," then it is *erratic. Invariable* and *consistent* mean "never changing," which is the opposite of "unpredictable." If the watershed can be used for tourists and residents as a recreational substitute, then the community members' concerns were alleviated, or *assuaged.*

15. D: *Aggrandize* is the correct answer because "adding excessive details" to reality would make reality greater than it really is. *Propitiate* is incorrect because one wouldn't try to "win the favor of" reality, nor is *precipitate* the correct answer, which means to instigate something. *Exacerbate* is more likely to fit, although the word implies a negative connotation rather than "adding excessive details." *Imitate* doesn't make sense within the context because "adding excessive details" would mean to go beyond reality, not to imitate it.

16. B: The answer *burgeoning* means to grow rapidly, which is an appropriate name for a field where "researchers are contributing significant findings to Fortune 500 research." The terms *diminishing, disparaging,* and *floundering* all indicate a lessening or a failing, and thus do not fit into the sentence. *Ambiguous* means open to more than one meaning, which negates the context of surety and growth.

Reading Comprehension

17. C, E: Choice *A* is incorrect because the seaport is noted as "thriving"; also, the slave trading companies were noted as being "lucrative." Choice *B* is incorrect because the slave traders actually built both office structures and slave holding buildings in downtown Alexandria; there is no mention of renting, or of landlords. Choice *D* is incorrect because the Bruin Slave Jail is not open to the public. Choice *C* is correct because Joseph Bruin bought hundreds of slaves during the years 1844 to 1861. Choice *E* is correct because the passage notes that the offices and slave holding units were open until the end of the Civil War.

18. A: Choices *B, C, D,* and *E* can all be regarded as false based on the information provided in the passage. Choice *A* contains information provided in the passage; therefore, the statement is true. Choice *B* is false because the passage infers that Joseph Bruin was notorious as a slave trader; in fact, two sisters tried to run away from Joseph Bruin. Choice *C* is false because the slave pen was not four stories high; the passage specifically noted that the slave pen was two stories high. Choice *D* is false because the passage does not refer to Union or Confederate soldiers, and the Bruin Slave Jail was what became the Fairfax County courthouse. Choice *E* is false because there is no information in the passage that indicates that literature, like *Uncle Tom's Cabin*, was preserved by the Northern Virginia Urban League.

19. C, D: Choice *A* is false, based on the passage statement that Alexandria was founded in 1749. Choice *B* is false because the passage does not suggest that Harriet Beecher Stowe was a slave; rather, the passage states that Stowe was the author of *Uncle Tom's Cabin*. Choice *C* is true; the passage claims that northern abolitionists tried to save two Christian slave sisters from a fate of prostitution. Choice *D* is true based on the information found in the passage. Choice *E* is false; the town of Annapolis is not cited in the passage.

20. C: The purpose of the passage is to shed light on the history of Joseph Bruin's Slave Jail and what became of it. Choice *A* is incorrect because while the two sisters are mentioned in the story to provide details, they are not the main purpose of the story. Choice *B* is incorrect because while the beginning of the story contains the information about the town and its slave business, this answer option leaves out the fact that the passage is focused on one slave jail in particular and omits anything about the conclusion of the passage, which is actually key in the main focus of the passage—how Joseph Bruin's Slave Jail came about and what became of it. Choice *D* is incorrect because the point of the passage is not about where the historical Bruin Slave Jail currently stands, but the history behind it.

21. B: The speaker's salutation is one from an entertainer to his audience and uses the friendly language to connect to his audience before a serious speech. Recall in the first paragraph that the speaker is there to "accompany [the audience] . . . through one of my little Christmas books," making him an author there to entertain the crowd with his own writing. The speech preceding the reading is the passage itself, and, as the tone indicates, a serious speech addressing the "working man." Although the passage speaks of employers and employees, the speaker himself is not an employer of the audience, so Choice *A* is incorrect. Choice *C* is also incorrect, as the salutation is not used ironically, but sincerely, as the speech addresses the well-being of the crowd. Choice *D* is incorrect because the speech is not given by a politician, but by a writer.

22. B: Choice *A* is incorrect because that is the speaker's *first* desire, not his second. Choices *C* and *D* are tricky because the language of both of these is mentioned after the word *second*. However, the speaker doesn't get to the second wish until the next sentence. Choices *C* and *D* are merely prepositions preparing for the statement of the main clause, Choice *B*, for the working man to have a say in his institution, which is designed for his benefit.

23. C: The speaker's tone can best be described as *confident and informed.* The speaker addresses the audience as "My good friends," and says, "I have no fear of being misunderstood," which implies confidence. Additionally, the speaker's knowledge of the proposal and topic can be seen in the text as well, especially in the second paragraph.

24. D: To provide credibility to the working man and share confidence in their ability to take on responsibilities if they are compensated appropriately. The speaker provides credibility by saying "he will stand by such an enterprise with the utmost of his patience," and displays their responsibilities by saying "he will feel his responsibility like an honest man."

25. A: The speaker says to "Erect in Birmingham a great Education Institution, properly educational." Choice *B* is close, but the speaker uses the name "Temple of Concord" in the passage as a metaphor, so this is incorrect. The other two choices aren't mentioned in the passage.

26. B: Readers should carefully focus their attention on the beginning of the passage to answer this series of questions. Even though the sentences may be worded a bit differently, all but one statement is true. It presents a false idea that descriptive details are not necessary until the climax of the story. Even if one does not read the passage, he or she probably knows that all good writing begins with descriptive details to develop the main theme the writer intends for the narrative.

27. C: This choice allows room for the fact that not all people who attempt to write a play will find it easy. If the writer follows the basic principles of narrative writing described in the passage, however, writing a play does not have to be an excruciating experience. None of the other options can be supported by points from the passage.

28. A, C: Choice *A* is true based on the sentence that reads, "Next, use dialogue to reveal the attitudes and personalities of each of the characters who have a key part in the unfolding story." Choice *C* is true based on the information that claims an image is like using a thousand words. Choice *B* is false because there is no drama with predictable progression. Choice *D* contradicts the point that the protagonist should experience self-discovery. Finally, Choice *E* is incorrect because all drama suggests some challenge for the characters to experience.

29. B: To suggest that a ten-minute play is accessible does not imply any timeline, nor does the passage mention how long a playwright spends with revisions and rewrites. So, Choice *A* is incorrect. Choice *B* is correct because of the opening statement that reads, "Learning how to write a ten-minute play may seem like a monumental task at first; but, if you follow a simple creative writing strategy, similar to writing a narrative story, you will be able to write a successful drama." None of the remaining choices are supported by points in the passage.

30. E: Note that the only element not mentioned in the passage is the style feature that is part of a narrative writer's tool kit. It is not to say that ten-minute plays do not have style. The correct answer denotes only that the element of style was not illustrated in this particular passage.

31. A, D: The passage references statements made by the World Bank in 1995 at the end of the first paragraph and in the middle of the second. The first reference says that state-owned enterprises "remain an important obstacle to better economic performance," and the second reference says the "World Bank recommended that SOEs be corporatized under commercial law and issued guidance." Thus, Choices *A* and *D* are the correct answers. Although the World Bank is probably discussing developing countries, they are not mentioned in the statements quoted in the passage, so Choice *B* is incorrect. Choice *C* is contradicted by the rest of the passage and never mentioned in connection with statements issued by the World Bank. While the passage discusses studies similar to what's described in Choice *E*, they are not included in the World Bank's statements.

32. B: The passage repeatedly mentions disputes over privatization, including inconclusive studies, scholars refuting the World Bank's statements about state-owned enterprises, and differences between free market advocates who want to "unleash" the private sector and the World Bank's more gradual approach. Thus, Choice *B* is the correct answer. Choice *A* is incorrect because "always" is too strong. The studies are inconclusive and have yielded conflicting results. Choice *C* is incorrect for similar reasons. Although the studies in this passage are criticized, it's too much to say economic studies in general are always subject to such criticism. The World Bank recommends that state-owned enterprises be privatized in accordance with commercial law, but that doesn't necessarily mean those enterprises violate commercial law, so Choice *D* is incorrect. Nowhere in the passage does it say the World Bank holds the power to intervene in economies; its statements are referred to as recommendations. Thus, Choice *E* is incorrect.

33. D, E: The passage states that state-owned enterprises have a "pervasive presence" in the global economy, and the World Bank includes competition and corporate governance free of political interference in its five preconditions for successful privatization. Therefore, Choices *D* and *E* are the correct answers. The empirical research is inconclusive but, if anything, it leans toward the opposite of what's described in Choice *A*. Influences on the World Bank's policies and popular support are never mentioned in the passage; therefore, Choices *B* and *C* are incorrect.

34. C: The author's conclusion is that "SOEs are an entity to be considered and managed in the pursuit of stability." As such, it can be inferred that the author supports the World Bank's measured approach of implementing privatization gradually to avoid the type of hasty action advocated by free market enthusiasts. Thus, Choice *C* is the correct answer. The author believes the market is the best allocator of resources, but it's unclear whether the author thinks private enterprises will always outperform state-owned enterprises, so this can't be the conclusion. Thus, Choice *A* is incorrect. The author would agree with Choices *B*, *D*, and *E*; however, all three are incorrect because they don't reflect the author's emphasis on stability.

35. A: The purpose is to inform the reader about what assault is and how it is committed. Choice *B* is incorrect because the passage does not state that assault is a lesser form of lethal force, only that an assault can use lethal force, or alternatively, lethal force can be utilized to counter a dangerous assault. Choices *C* and *D* are incorrect because the passage is informative and does not have a set agenda. Finally, Choice *E* is incorrect because although the author uses an example in order to explain assault, it is not indicated that this is the author's personal account.

36. C: The situation of the man who is attacked in an alley by another man with a knife would most merit the use of lethal force. If the man being attacked used self-defense by lethal force, it would not be considered illegal. The presence of a deadly weapon indicates mal-intent and because the individual is isolated in an alley, lethal force in self-defense may be the only way to preserve his life. Choices *A* and *B* can be ruled out because in these situations, no one is in danger of immediate death or bodily harm by someone else. Choice *D* is an assault that does exhibit intent to harm, but this situation isn't severe enough to merit lethal force; there is no intent to kill. Choice *E* is incorrect because this is a vehicular accident, and the driver did not intend to hit and injure the other driver.

37. B: As discussed in the second passage, there are several forms of assault, like assault with a deadly weapon, verbal assault, or threatening posture or language. Choice *A* is incorrect because lethal force and assault are separate as indicated by the passages. Choice *C* is incorrect because anyone is capable of assault; the author does not state that one group of people cannot commit assault. Choice *D* is incorrect because assault is never justified. Self-defense resulting in lethal force can be justified. Choice *E* is incorrect because the author does mention what the charges are on assaults; therefore, we cannot assume that they are more or less than unnecessary use of force charges.

38. D: The use of lethal force is not evaluated on the intent of the user but rather the severity of the primary attack that warranted self-defense. This statement most undermines the last part of the passage because it directly contradicts how the law evaluates the use of lethal force. Choices *A*, *B*, and *E* are stated in the paragraph, and therefore do not undermine the explanation from the author. Choice *C* does not necessarily undermine the passage, but it does not support the passage either. It is more of an opinion that does not strengthen or weaken the explanation.

39. C: An assault with deadly intent can lead to an individual using lethal force to preserve their well-being. Choice *C* is correct because it clearly establishes what both assault and lethal force are and gives the specific way in which the two concepts meet. Choice *A* is incorrect because lethal force doesn't necessarily result in assault. This is also why Choice *B* is incorrect. Not all assaults would necessarily be life-threatening to the point where lethal force is needed for self-defense. Choice *D* is compelling but ultimately too vague; the statement touches on aspects of the two ideas but fails to present the concrete way in which the two are connected to each other. Choice *E* is incorrect because it contradicts the information in the passage (that assault with deadly intent can lead to an individual using lethal force).

40. A: Both passages open by defining a legal concept and then describing situations in order to further explain the concept. Choice *D* is incorrect because while the passages utilize examples to help explain the concepts discussed, the author doesn't indicate that they are specific court cases. It's also clear that the passages don't open with examples, but instead, begin by defining the terms addressed in each passage. This eliminates Choice *B* and ultimately reveals Choice *A* to be the correct answer. Choice *A* accurately outlines the way both passages are structured. Because the passages follow a near identical structure, the rest of the choices can easily be ruled out.

41. E: Intent is very important for determining both lethal force and assault; intent is examined by both parties and helps determine the severity of the issue. Choices *A*, *B*, and *C* are incorrect because it is clear in both passages that intent is a prevailing theme in both lethal force and assault. Choice *D* is compelling, but if a person uses lethal force to defend themselves, the intent of the defender is also examined in order to help determine if there was excessive force used. Choice *E* is correct because it states that intent is important for determining both lethal force and assault, and that intent is used to gauge the severity of the issues. Remember, just as lethal force can escalate to excessive use of force, there are different kinds of assault. Intent dictates several different forms of assault.

Sentence Equivalence

42. A, C: The key word in this sentence is "but," a conjunction that signals that something will be contrasted with something else. In this sentence the word "motivated" suggests a positive mood, so the answer words should be a switch from positive to negative. Therefore, because *energized*, *vigorous*, *indefatigable*, and *enterprising* are lively words, the best choices to complete the thought without changing the meaning are *lackadaisical* and *lethargic*.

43. D, F: Even if readers don't know what *cacophony* means, they can tell that four of the words are closely related. Readers should try to eliminate what they know in order to focus on the remaining words. If two notes are not in perfect accord with each other, they are demonstrating dissonance. The words *accord*, *harmony*, *concordance*, and *composition* have a relationship with each other; therefore, the two words that mean the same and maintain the meaning of the sentence are *cacophony* and *dissonance*.

44. B, E: Knowing that a thief is part of the equation suggests that he would leave the scene of the crime; therefore, *absconded* and *bolted*, which mean "leave in a hurry," most accurately complete the meaning of the sentence. Readers may be able to find two other synonyms, however, that do not suggest leaving the scene of the crime.

45. C, D: Several of the choices fit nicely in the sentence; but, readers should complete the sentence with two synonyms that best fit the meaning the writer intended. *Astute* means "intelligent"; *apt* is close, but it means "relevant," which is not a synonym of intelligent. *Mediocre* and *middling* seem to mean the same thing, but they don't work with an immature writing style. Therefore, *banal* and *trite* are the best choices for this sentence.

46. B, D: If readers understand that "dubious" implies a challenge that the politicians would like to avoid, they will see that *obscuring* and *obfuscating* work the best to maintain the idea of the sentence. *Pontificating* suggests preaching. *Discussing* and *confabulating* could be synonyms; however, they do not fit with the negative word *dubious*. *Explicating* suggests a levelheaded explanation.

47. B, D: The key word to understand how to fill in the blank in this sentence is "pleasure." Several of the choices take away the meaning when inserted. Therefore, the best phrases needed to complete the idea that modeling is pleasurable but requires sacrifices are *accede to* and *acquiesce to*.

48. B, C: Because the students were unprepared, two words that imply a negative emotion would be appropriate to complete the sentence. *Feint* suggests a sham or pretense, *diatribe* is a tirade, and *enmity* and *exuberance* do not complete the meaning of the sentence.

49. A, D: In order for the debate team to win, their opponents must not be as intelligent or quick-witted as their own team members. So *vacuous* and *fatuous* are the synonyms that work best. *Fatuous* means "dense" or "dim-witted," while *vacuous* means "lacking intelligence."

50. A, F: Without the word "holiday," several of the choices might work to complete the meaning of the sentence. However, the best two synonyms that mean "overly emotional" or "sentimental" are *maudlin* and *quixotic*. If readers are not sure which words to pick, they can use the process of elimination. A *nefarious* or *moribund* movie would not be uplifting. Even though a *valorous* movie could be a holiday movie theme, it does not have a matching synonym as a choice.

GRE Verbal Practice Test #2

Text Completion

Select the best word from the corresponding column of choices that most clearly completes the passage:

1. The challenge the pollsters found in working with rural community populations was that the poll results were taken from a (i) _____ group. Therefore, the findings were often (ii) _____ because the participants were very similar in nature.

Blank (i)	Blank (ii)
a. Heterogeneous	d. Skewed
b. Disparate	e. Valid
c. Homogeneous	f. Accurate

2. The board members wrote in their public (i) _____ that Mr. Albert Stanley, the chairman of the UERL (Underground Electric Railways Company of London), would always be remembered for his outstanding innovations using public relations to increase the company's profit margins.

Blank (i)
a. Memoirs
b. Panegyric
c. Meditations
d. Reproofs
e. Obloquy

3. Artificial intelligence is on the brink of a major breakthrough in communication. As few as five years ago, artificial intelligence could not (i) _____ process verbal command. Now, artificial intelligence immediately recognizes the (ii) _____ of what someone is saying at a minimum. With time, it's expected that machines will equal and perhaps even (iii) _____ humanity's communication skills.

Blank (i)	Blank (ii)	Blank (iii)
a. Chronologically	d. Aesthetic	g. Aggregate
b. Effectively	e. Coda	h. Mollify
c. Zealously	f. Gist	i. Surpass

4. John was running out of time to study before his big test. To maximize his chances of passing, John began exclusively concentrating on the main topics instead of the (i) _____ material.

Blank (i)
a. fatuous
b. specious
c. tangential

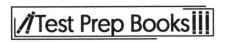

5. Grassroots organizers have become increasingly (i) _____ by the electoral process. Despite raising money from more donors and doing exponentially more community outreach every election cycle, they've been repeatedly steamrolled by candidates funded by billionaires. Consequently, some of the organizers have started to consider (ii) _____ support for radical action to circumvent the electoral process.

Blank (i)	Blank (ii)
a. appeased	d. fluctuating
b. oscillated	e. fomenting
c. vexed	f. forestalling

6. Juan is a talented painter best known for his use of (i) _____. His most famous painting depicts American colonialists huddled around a television watching cartoons as the Revolutionary War wages in a field visible through an open window. This work (ii) _____ confusion and horror in viewers who don't understand why the colonialists are watching television as their countrymen are fighting and dying for freedom.

Blank (i)	Blank (ii)
a. anachronism	d. abates
b. hyperbole	e. elicits
c. irony	f. obviates

7. Jacob is a terrific team leader. Even on short notice, Jacob is able to (i) _____ his team to produce rapid results. In contrast, Lisa is (ii) _____. Whenever confronted with a difficult situation, she becomes angry and unapproachable.

Blank (i)	Blank (ii)
a. enervate	d. irascible
b. galvanize	e. tortuous
c. venerate	f. zealous

8. There are several key differences between the United States and Scandinavia. First, the United States is a multicultural country of immigrants, while Scandinavia is mostly (i) _____. Second, the mainstream political (ii) _____ leans farther to the right in the United States than in Scandinavia. Third, the United States carries out a more (iii) _____ and interventionist foreign policy than Scandinavia.

Blank (i)	Blank (ii)	Blank (iii)
a. ambiguous	d. cacophony	g. ambivalent
b. homogeneous	e. hegemony	h. bellicose
c. sedulous	f. ideology	i. timorous

9. Tensions were running high between two employees, so the employer pulled each employee aside separately in the hopes of (i) _____ them. The employer needed the pair to stop (ii) _____ each other before a workable solution could be (iii) _____.

Blank (i)	Blank (ii)	Blank (iii)
a. placating	d. denigrating	g. effectuated
b. prevaricating	e. disabusing	h. exculpated
c. refuting	f. venerating	i. extrapolated

10. We learned that, due to his uncertainty on the subject, the politician was (i) _____ about the president's role in (ii) _____ in the Yemen civil war. On the other hand, our state senator was shocked by the (iii) _____ decision to help Saudi Arabia.

Blank (i)	Blank (ii)	Blank (iii)
a. ebullient	d. refraining	g. impetuous
b. ambivalent	e. renouncing	h. temperate
c. hapless	f. engaging	i. impassive

11. The chief police of Hilltop, Indiana was (i) _____ to patrolman due to his inability to (ii) _____ the city's crime rates.

Blank (i)	Blank (ii)
a. relegated	d. escalate
b. endorsed	e. mitigate
c. promoted	f. trasmit

12. Because of her increase in sales, the writer was able to contribute to her two favorite charities, causing her to have a (i) _____ year.

Blank (i)
a. noxious
b. munificent
c. inveterate
d. inimical
e. fallacious

13. The team member (i) _____ to the suggestions of his coworker when he found out that she had singlehandedly (ii) _____ the Peterson account last year.

Blank (i)	Blank (ii)
a. admonished	d. procured
b. swooned	e. aggregated
c. acceded	f. precipitated

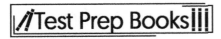

14. The island was (i) _____ with turmoil due to its recent hurricane destruction.

Blank (i)
a. sanguine
b. obdurate
c. mawkish
d. prudent
e. rife

15. While camping, we were (i) _____ of any sounds we heard during the night because of the recent bear attack. However, we knew that the night rangers were (ii) _____ of any threat to the campers while they were on night patrol.

Blank (i)	Blank (ii)
a. leery	d. cognizant
b. elated	e. oblivious
c. assuaged	f. quarantined

16. The captain's (i) _____ was that the storm would be much worse than the authorities predicted, so he turned the boat around and headed for shore.

Blank (i)
a. dialect
b. visage
c. premonition
d. psyche
e. prestige

Reading Comprehension

Questions 17–22 are based on the following passage.

Dana Gioia argues in his article that poetry is dying, now little more than a limited art form confined to academic and college settings. Of course poetry remains healthy in the academic setting, but the idea of poetry being limited to this academic subculture is a stretch. New technology and social networking alone have contributed to poets and other writers' work being shared across the world. YouTube has emerged to be a major asset to poets, allowing live performances to be streamed to billions of users. Even now, poetry continues to grow and voice topics that are relevant to the culture of our time. Poetry is not in the spotlight as it may have been in earlier times, but it's still a relevant art form that continues to expand in scope and appeal.

Furthermore, Gioia's argument does not account for live performances of poetry. Not everyone has taken a poetry class or enrolled in university—but most everyone is online. The Internet is a perfect launching point to get all creative work out there. An example of this was the performance of Buddy Wakefield's *Hurling Crowbirds at Mockingbars*. Wakefield is a well-known poet who has published several collections of contemporary poetry. One of my favorite works by Wakefield is *Crowbirds*, specifically his performance at New York University in 2009. Although

58

his reading was a campus event, views of his performance online number in the thousands. His poetry attracted people outside of the university setting.

Naturally, the poem's popularity can be attributed both to Wakefield's performance and the quality of his writing. *Crowbirds* touches on themes of core human concepts such as faith, personal loss, and growth. These are not ideas that only poets or students of literature understand, but all human beings: "You acted like I was hurling crowbirds at mockingbars / and abandoned me for not making sense. / Evidently, I don't experience things as rationally as you do" (Wakefield 15-17). Wakefield weaves together a complex description of the perplexed and hurt emotions of the speaker undergoing a separation from a romantic interest. The line "You acted like I was hurling crowbirds at mockingbars" conjures up an image of someone confused, seemingly out of their mind . . . or in the case of the speaker, passionately trying to grasp at a relationship that is fading. The speaker is looking back and finding the words that described how he wasn't making sense. This poem is particularly human and gripping in its message, but the entire effect of the poem is enhanced through the physical performance.

At its core, poetry is about addressing issues/ideas in the world. Part of this is also addressing the perspectives that are exiguously considered. Although the platform may look different, poetry continues to have a steady audience due to the emotional connection the poet shares with the audience.

Select only one answer choice:

17. Which one of the following best explains how the passage is organized?
    a. The author begins with a long definition of the main topic, and then proceeds to prove how that definition has changed over the course of modernity.
    b. The author presents a puzzling phenomenon and uses the rest of the passage to showcase personal experiences in order to explain it.
    c. The author contrasts two different viewpoints, then builds a case showing preference for one over the other.
    d. The passage is an analysis of another theory that the author has no stake in.
    e. The passage is a summary of a main topic from its historical beginnings to its contemplated end.

Select only one answer choice:

18. The author of the passage would likely agree most with which of the following?
    a. Buddy Wakefield is a genius and is considered at the forefront of modern poetry.
    b. Poetry is not irrelevant; it is an art form that adapts to the changing time while containing its core elements.
    c. Spoken word is the zenith of poetic forms and the premier style of poetry in this decade.
    d. Poetry is on the verge of vanishing from our cultural consciousness.
    e. Poetry is a writing art. While poetry performances are useful for introducing poems, the act of reading a poem does not contribute to the piece overall.

Select only one answer choice:

19. Which one of the following words, if substituted for the word *exiguously* in the last paragraph, would LEAST change the meaning of the sentence?
    a. Indolently
    b. Inaudibly
    c. Interminably
    d. Infrequently
    e. Impecunious

Select only one answer choice:

20. Which of the following is most closely analogous to the author's opinion of Buddy Wakefield's performance in relation to modern poetry?
    a. Someone's refusal to accept that the Higgs Boson will validate the Standard Model.
    b. An individual's belief that soccer will lose popularity within the next fifty years.
    c. A professor's opinion that poetry contains the language of the heart, while fiction contains the language of the mind.
    d. An individual's assertion that video game violence was the cause of the Columbine shootings.
    e. A student's insistence that psychoanalysis is a subset of modern psychology.

Select only one answer choice:

21. What is the primary purpose of the passage?
    a. To educate readers on the development of poetry and describe the historical implications of poetry in media.
    b. To disprove Dana Gioia's stance that poetry is becoming irrelevant and is only appreciated in academia.
    c. To inform readers of the brilliance of Buddy Wakefield and to introduce them to other poets that have influenced contemporary poetry.
    d. To prove that Gioia's article does have some truth to it and to shed light on its relevance to modern poetry.
    e. To recount the experience of watching a live poetry performance and to look forward to future performances.

Select only one answer choice:

22. What is the author's main reason for including the quote in the passage?
    a. To give an example of speaking meter, the writing style of spoken word poets.
    b. To demonstrate that people are still writing poetry even if the medium has changed in current times.
    c. To prove that poets still have an audience to write for even if the audience looks different than from centuries ago.
    d. To illustrate the complex themes poets continue to address, which still draw listeners and appreciation.
    e. To open up opportunity to disprove Gioia's views.

Questions 23–27 are based on the following passage:

Becoming a successful leader in today's industry, government, and nonprofit sectors requires more than a high intelligence quotient (IQ). Emotional Intelligence (EI) includes developing the ability to know one's own emotions, to regulate impulses and emotions, and to use interpersonal communication skills with ease while dealing with other people. A combination of knowledge, skills, abilities, and mature emotional intelligence (EI) reflects the most effective leadership recipe. Successful leaders sharpen more than their talents and IQ levels; they practice the basic features of emotional intelligence. Some of the hallmark traits of a competent, emotionally intelligent leader include self-efficacy, drive, determination, collaboration, vision, humility, and openness to change. An unsuccessful leader exhibits opposite leadership traits: unclear directives, inconsistent vision and planning strategies, disrespect for followers, incompetence, and an uncompromising transactional leadership style. There are ways to develop emotional intelligence for the person who wants to improve his or her leadership style. For example, an emotionally intelligent leader creates an affirmative environment by incorporating collaborative activities, using professional development training for employee self-awareness, communicating clearly about the organization's vision, and developing a variety of resources for working with emotions. Building relationships outside the institution with leadership coaches and with professional development trainers can also help leaders who want to grow their leadership success. Leaders in today's work environment need to strive for a combination of skill, knowledge, and mature emotional intelligence to lead followers to success and to promote the vision and mission of their respective institutions.

Select only one answer choice:

23. The passage suggests that the term *emotional intelligence (EI)* can be defined as which of the following?
  a. A combination of knowledge, skills, abilities, and mature emotional intelligence reflects the most effective EI leadership recipe.
  b. An emotionally intelligent leader creates an affirmative environment by incorporating collaborative activities, using professional development training for employee self-awareness, communicating clearly about the organization's vision, and developing a variety of resources for working with emotions.
  c. EI includes developing the ability to know one's own emotions, to regulate impulses and emotions, and to use interpersonal communication skills with ease while dealing with other people.
  d. Becoming a successful leader in today's industry, government, and nonprofit sectors requires more than a high IQ.
  e. An EI leader exhibits the following leadership traits: unclear directives, inconsistent vision and planning strategies, disrespect for followers, incompetence, and uncompromising transactional leadership style.

Select only one answer choice:

24. Based on the information in the passage, a successful leader must have a high EI quotient.
   a. The above statement can be supported by the fact that Daniel Goldman conducted a scientific study.
   b. The above statement can be supported by the example that emotionally intelligent people are highly successful leaders.
   c. The above statement is not supported by the passage.
   d. The above statement is supported by the illustration that claims, "Leaders in today's work environment need to strive for a combination of skill, knowledge, and mature emotional intelligence to lead followers to success and to promote the vision and mission of their respective institutions."
   e. The above statement can be inferred because emotionally intelligent people obviously make successful leaders.

Select only one answer choice:

25. According to the passage, some of the characteristics of an unsuccessful leader include which of the following?
   a. Talent, IQ level, and abilities
   b. Humility, knowledge, and skills
   c. Loud, demeaning actions toward female employees
   d. Outdated technological resources and strategies
   e. Transactional leadership style

Select only one answer choice:

26. According to the passage, which of the following must be true?
   a. The leader exhibits a healthy work/life balance lifestyle.
   b. The leader is uncompromising in transactional directives for all employees, regardless of status.
   c. The leader learns to strategize using future trends analysis to create a five-year plan.
   d. The leader uses a combination of skill, knowledge, and mature reasoning to make decisions.
   e. The leader continually tries to improve his or her EI test quotient by studying the intelligence quotient of other successful leaders.

Consider each of the choices separately and select all that apply:

27. According to the passage, which of the following choices are true?
   a. To be successful, leaders in the nonprofit sector need to develop emotional intelligence.
   b. It is not necessary for military leaders to develop emotional intelligence because they prefer a transactional leadership style.
   c. Leadership coaches can add value to someone who is developing his or her emotional intelligence.
   d. Humility is a valued character value; however, it is not necessarily a trademark of an emotionally intelligent leader.
   e. If a leader does not have the level of emotional intelligence required for a certain job, he or she is capable of increasing emotional intelligence.

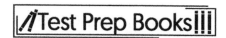

Questions 28–32 are based upon the following passage:

Three years ago, I think there were not many bird-lovers in the United States, who believed it possible to prevent the total extinction of both egrets from our fauna. All the known rookeries accessible to plume-hunters had been totally destroyed. Two years ago, the secret discovery of several small, hidden colonies prompted William Dutcher, President of the National Association of Audubon Societies, and Mr. T. Gilbert Pearson, Secretary, to attempt the protection of those colonies. With a fund contributed for the purpose, wardens were hired and duly commissioned. As previously stated, one of those wardens was shot dead in cold blood by a plume hunter. The task of guarding swamp rookeries from the attacks of money-hungry desperadoes to whom the accursed plumes were worth their weight in gold, is a very chancy proceeding. There is now one warden in Florida who says that "before they get my rookery they will first have to get me."

Thus far the protective work of the Audubon Association has been successful. Now there are twenty colonies, which contain all told, about 5,000 egrets and about 120,000 herons and ibises which are guarded by the Audubon wardens. One of the most important is on Bird Island, a mile out in Orange Lake, central Florida, and it is ably defended by Oscar E. Baynard. To-day, the plume hunters who do not dare to raid the guarded rookeries are trying to study out the lines of flight of the birds, to and from their feeding-grounds, and shoot them in transit. Their motto is—"Anything to beat the law, and get the plumes." It is there that the state of Florida should take part in the war.

The success of this campaign is attested by the fact that last year a number of egrets were seen in eastern Massachusetts—for the first time in many years. And so to-day the question is, can the wardens continue to hold the plume-hunters at bay?

Excerpt from *Our Vanishing Wildlife* by William T. Hornaday

Select only one answer choice:

28. The author's use of first person pronoun in the following text does NOT have which of the following effects?

Three years ago, I think there were not many bird-lovers in the United States, who believed it possible to prevent the total extinction of both egrets from our fauna.

a. The phrase *I think* acts as a sort of hedging, where the author's tone is less direct and/or absolute.
b. It allows the reader to more easily connect with the author.
c. It encourages the reader to empathize with the egrets.
d. It distances the reader from the text by overemphasizing the story.

Select only one answer choice:

29. What purpose does the quote serve at the end of the first paragraph?
a. The quote shows proof of a hunter threatening one of the wardens.
b. The quote lightens the mood by illustrating the colloquial language of the region.
c. The quote provides an example of a warden protecting one of the colonies.
d. The quote provides much needed comic relief in the form of a joke.

Select only one answer choice:

30. What is on Bird Island?
    a. Hunters selling plumes
    b. An important bird colony
    c. Bird Island Battle between the hunters and the wardens
    d. An important egret with unique plumes

Select only one answer choice:

31. What is the main purpose of the passage?
    a. To persuade the audience to act in preservation of the bird colonies
    b. To show the effect hunting egrets has had on the environment
    c. To argue that the preservation of bird colonies has had a negative impact on the environment
    d. To demonstrate the success of the protective work of the Audubon Association

Select only one answer choice:

32. According to the passage, why are hunters trying to study the lines of flight of the birds?
    a. To study ornithology, one must know the lines of flight that birds take.
    b. To help wardens preserve the lives of the birds
    c. To have a better opportunity to hunt the birds
    d. To build their homes under the lines of flight because they believe it brings good luck

Questions 33–37 are based upon the following passage:

Insects as a whole are preeminently creatures of the land and the air. This is shown not only by the possession of wings by a vast majority of the class, but by the mode of breathing to which reference has already been made, a system of branching air-tubes carrying atmospheric air with its combustion-supporting oxygen to all the insect's tissues. The air gains access to these tubes through a number of paired air-holes or spiracles, arranged segmentally in series.

It is of great interest to find that, nevertheless, a number of insects spend much of their time under water. This is true of not a few in the perfect winged state, as for example aquatic beetles and water-bugs ('boatmen' and 'scorpions') which have some way of protecting their spiracles when submerged, and, possessing usually the power of flight, can pass on occasion from pond or stream to upper air. But it is advisable in connection with our present subject to dwell especially on some insects that remain continually under water till they are ready to undergo their final moult and attain the winged state, which they pass entirely in the air. The preparatory instars of such insects are aquatic; the adult instar is aerial. All may-flies, dragon-flies, and caddis-flies, many beetles and two-winged flies, and a few moths thus divide their life-story between the water and the air. For the present we confine attention to the Stone-flies, the May-flies, and the Dragon-flies, three well-known orders of insects respectively called by systematists the Plecoptera, the Ephemeroptera and the Odonata.

In the case of many insects that have aquatic larvae, the latter are provided with some arrangement for enabling them to reach atmospheric air through the surface-film of the water. But the larva of a stone-fly, a dragon-fly, or a may-fly is adapted more completely

than these for aquatic life; it can, by means of gills of some kind, breathe the air dissolved in water.

This excerpt is from *The Life-Story of Insects* by Geo H. Carpenter

Select only one answer choice:

33. Which statement best details the central idea in this passage?
    a. It introduces certain insects that transition from water to air.
    b. It delves into entomology, especially where gills are concerned.
    c. It defines what constitutes as insects' breathing.
    d. It invites readers to have a hand in the preservation of insects.

Select only one answer choice:

34. What is the purpose of the first paragraph in relation to the second paragraph?
    a. The first paragraph serves as a cause, and the second paragraph serves as an effect.
    b. The first paragraph serves as a contrast to the second.
    c. The first paragraph is a description for the argument in the second paragraph.
    d. The first and second paragraphs are merely presented in a sequence.

Select only one answer choice:

35. Which of the statements reflect information that one could reasonably infer based on the author's tone?
    a. The author's tone is persuasive and attempts to call the audience to action.
    b. The author's tone is passionate due to excitement over the subject and personal narrative.
    c. The author's tone is informative and exhibits interest in the subject of the study.
    d. The author's tone is somber, depicting some anger at the state of insect larvae.

Select only one answer choice:

36. The last paragraph indicates that the author believes
    a. That the stonefly, dragonfly, and mayfly larvae are better prepared to live beneath the water because they have gills that allow them to do so.
    b. That the stonefly is different from the mayfly because the stonefly can breathe underwater and the mayfly can only breathe above water.
    c. That the dragonfly is a unique species in that its larvae lives mostly underwater for most of its young life.
    d. That the stonefly larvae can breathe only by reaching the surface film of the water.

Select only one answer choice:

37. According to the passage, why are insects as a whole preeminently creatures of the land and the air?
    a. Because insects are born on land but eventually end up adapting to life underwater for the rest of their adult lives.
    b. Because most insects have legs made for walking on land and tube-like structures on their bellies for skimming the water.
    c. Because a vast majority of insects have wings and also have the ability to breathe underwater.
    d. Because most insects have a propulsion method specifically designed for underwater use, but they can only breathe on land.

Questions 38–41 are based on the following passage:

Scholars who have examined how national leaders historically craft public speeches in response to accusations of offensive words or deeds conclude that such officials generally rely upon one of two recurrent strategic approaches. The first of these is apologia, which William Benoit and Susan Brinson define as "a recurring type of discourse designed to restore face, image, or reputation after an alleged or suspected wrongdoing," which occurs during many apologies. The second is reconciliation, which John Hatch defines as "a dialogic rhetorical process of healing between the parties."

Speakers using apologia strive to restore their own credibility and remove any perception they might be guilty of involvement in the transgression. Speakers seeking reconciliation are interested in restoring dialogue instead of pursuing the purposes of shifting blame, denying charges, or some other form of blame avoidance or image repair.

Apologia focuses on short-term gains achievable by regaining favor with audiences already predisposed to the speaker's arguments. Reconciliation, by contrast, has a goal of understanding the long-term processes of image restoration and mutual respect between the aggrieved and the transgressor. Attempts at credible reconciliation utilize symbols of reunion to demonstrate that the aggrieved has *genuinely* granted the forgiveness sought by the offender. Visual images freeze the moment of genuine forgiveness and, when replayed in the online environment, carry forward the steps of reunification into perpetuity.

Not all offending images circulating in the online environment warrant a visual response or even an apology by national leaders. Nevertheless, failure to respond to the small number of potent images of transgressions that share characteristics qualifying them for continued recirculation in future propaganda efforts could be a costly mistake. Reconciliation provides a fruitful choice, as its long-term goals match the ongoing need to handle ever-circulating images that offend.

Visual Propaganda and Extremism the Online Environment, edited by Carol K. Winkler and Cori E. Dauber (2014), published by the Strategic Studies Institute (Department of Defense), "Visual Reconciliation as Strategy of Response to Offending Images" by Carol K. Winkler, excerpted from pages 63-64, 71-72, and 74

Consider each of the choices separately and select all that apply:

38. Which statement(s) accurately describes the difference between apologia and reconciliation based on the passage?
    a. Apologia is a dialogic rhetorical process that involves healing, while reconciliation seeks to restore the image of a party suspected of wrongdoing.
    b. Reconciliation utilizes symbols to demonstrate forgiveness, while apologia is always delivered in writing.
    c. Apologia is more effective in the short term, while reconciliation is more useful for improving relationships in the long term.
    d. Reconciliation seeks to open channels of communication, while apologia is more closely related to shifting blame and rehabilitating credibility.
    e. Apologia requires the aggrieved party's forgiveness, while reconciliation is a strategic approach to delivering visual responses.

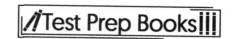

Select only one answer choice:

39. Based on the passage, which statement(s) can be properly inferred?
    a. National leaders should never apologize because reconciliation is always the superior option.
    b. Reconciliation is more effective than apologia because it is not self-serving.
    c. Apologia and reconciliation are most effective when delivered together.
    d. Apologia and reconciliation only function properly in the online environment.
    e. Maintaining a positive national image is an important part of governance.

Consider each of the choices separately and select all that apply:

40. Which statement(s) describes a feature of reconciliation?
    a. Reconciliation involves restoring dialogue and repairing relationships in the long term.
    b. Reconciliation leverages symbols of reunion to demonstrate that the aggrieved has genuinely granted the forgiveness sought by the offender.
    c. Reconciliation focuses on shifting blame, denying charges, restoring credibility, or otherwise repairing the offender's image.
    d. Reconciliation should be used when the audience is already predisposed to the speaker's argument
    e. Reconciliation prioritizes short-term gains over substantively altering the underlying relationship.

Select only one answer choice:

41. Which statement(s) describes how the author believes national leaders should respond to offending images circulating in the online environment?
    a. National leaders should censor all offending images and attack any group that disseminates propaganda.
    b. National leaders should conduct an anti-propaganda campaign to raise public awareness about the dangers of sensationalism.
    c. The circulation of offending images in online environments is inevitable but relatively harmless, so this phenomenon should be ignored.
    d. All offending images should be addressed with either apologia or reconciliation, depending on which is more appropriate based on context.
    e. Some offending images do not warrant any response, but for the ones that do reconciliation is the more appealing option due to its long-term impact.

Sentence Equivalence

Select the __two__ answer choices that can complete the sentence and create sentences that have complementary meaning.

42. During the ancient ceremony of death, the African tribe built several _____, lined up together, in order to burn their fallen warriors after battle.
    a. pyres
    b. bonfires
    c. pariahs
    d. juntas
    e. liens
    f. panoplies

43. The technology seminar's keynote speaker started out with simple terms, which grew more and more _____ as he continued the lecture.
   - a. lucid
   - b. esoteric
   - c. abstruse
   - d. acerbic
   - e. caustic
   - f. perspicacious

44. Miles Davis, the famous jazz legend, made a/an _____ impact on the development of jazz music because of his ability to make the sounds mimic the sounds of human voices.
   - a. incorrigible
   - b. viscous
   - c. ineradicable
   - d. sedulous
   - e. palpable
   - f. indelible

45. Four roommates were looking for a simple, affordable apartment near the school; however, the agent insisted on showing them apartments that were _____ and expensive.
   - a. portentous
   - b. extravagant
   - c. loquacious
   - d. austere
   - e. obsequious
   - f. palatial

46. A certain feeling of _____ descended on the group when they heard about the uncertain future of the start-up company where they worked; no one moved while the new information was presented during the meeting.
   - a. malaise
   - b. angst
   - c. chicanery
   - d. deference
   - e. quiescence
   - f. turpitude

47. The summer interns looked forward to working with the congressman, not knowing that he was also a _____.
   - a. tyro
   - b. zealot
   - c. savant
   - d. philanthropist
   - e. misogynist
   - f. novice

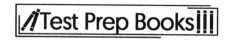

48. Much to the surprise of the senator, the interview questions focused on forgotten
_____, rather than on his impressive voting record.
    a. peccadilloes
    b. indiscretions
    c. efficacies
    d. anachronisms
    e. diatribes
    f. misnomers

49. The Prell shampoo commercials stayed in the minds of the viewers due to the
_____ movement of the pearl dropped into the golden bottle of premium, thick
shampoo. It became a classic advertisement in the 1970s.
    a. viscous
    b. ambrosial
    c. caustic
    d. ephemeral
    e. insular
    f. gradual

50. There was one particular NFL football player who consistently delivered abrupt and
_____ answers when the media approached him after the game.
    a. loquacious
    b. laconic
    c. verbose
    d. bombastic
    e. terse
    f. ranting

Answer Explanations #2

Text Completion

1. C, D: The key phrase for the first blank is "very similar." Go back to the first grouping of choices to find a word that has a relationship to the phrase "very similar." Readers will identify the word *homogeneous*, which means "the same." Then one can infer that the pollsters' results were not valid because of a grouping that did not have many variables. As readers look at the options for the second blank, they should think about the logical result of this poll. Being *accurate* is not an issue here. To be *valid* is also not quite the purpose of polling. The heavily biased results would be a problem for the pollsters.

2. B: One of the key words to help readers select the best choice in this sentence is "outstanding." There is a tone of praise and acclaim to the main idea promoted in the sentence. Readers can eliminate words that have a negative connotation, such as *reproofs* and *obloquy*. *Meditations* does not fit within the context of the passage. *Memoirs* might work; however, it does not complete the full meaning of providing public praise for Mr. Stanley.

3. B, F, I: Effectively (Choice *B*) means producing the desired result, and it's the best fit for Blank (i). The passage is describing a major breakthrough happening in the present day, and five years ago artificial intelligence was having a problem processing verbal commands. Chronology (Choice *A*) has to do with placing events in the correct order, and zealously (Choice *C*) means doing something with energy or enthusiasm. Thus, Choice *B* is the correct answer.

Gist (Choice *F*) is the main thrust of an idea without details, and that completes Blank (ii), which is describing a new development in artificial intelligence's ability to process verbal commands. Aesthetic (Choice *D*) is related to beauty, and coda (Choice *E*) is the concluding part of a musical piece or movement. Thus, Choice *F* is the correct answer.

Surpass (Choice *I*) fits Blank (iii) because the rest of the sentence is implying that artificial intelligence will at least equal humanity's communication skills, and surpass means to exceed. Aggregate (Choice *G*) is the combining of parts into a whole, and mollify (Choice *H*) means to soothe someone who is angry or anxious. Thus, Choice *I* is the correct answer.

4. C: John is running out of time and has chosen to concentrate on the main topics instead of some other material. So, Blank (i) should be something less important than those main topics. Tangential (Choice *C*) is something that's incidental or on the periphery, which fits this context. Fatuous (Choice *A*) is the second best answer choice because it can mean inane or pointless; however, fatuous connotes foolishness, so tangential is the better match. Specious (Choice *B*) means deceptively attractive— something that looks right but is really wrong—so it doesn't make sense that John would study specious material even if he had more time. Thus, Choice *C* is the correct answer.

5. C, E: The second sentence describes how grassroots organizers keep losing elections despite their best efforts. Vexed (Choice *C*) means feeling irritated, annoyed, or distressed, which accurately expresses the organizers' attitude toward the electoral process. Appeasing (Choice *A*) someone or something involves making concessions. In this context, oscillate (Choice *B*) would mean the organizers are alternating between favoring and opposing the electoral process. Thus, Choice *C* is correct.

Since the electoral process has vexed the organizers, Blank (ii) will express their desire to move away from that process, like actively supporting radical action. To foment (Choice *E*) is to instigate or promote, and this matches the organizers' desire to circumvent the electoral process by supporting radical action. Fluctuating (Choice *D*) refers to shifting one's position because of uncertainty, and forestalling (Choice *F*) means preemptively taking action to prevent or obstruct something, which is the opposite of what's intended here. Thus, Choice *E* is the correct answer.

6. A, E: The second sentence describes a panting depicting American colonialist watching television, which is a shocking image since television was invented more than a century after the American Revolution. Since this is Juan's most famous painting, it likely involves Juan's signature style, which is what's needed to complete Blank (i). Anachronism (Choice *A*) is something that stands out for being conspicuously placed in the wrong time period. Hyperbole (Choice *B*) is an exaggeration that serves some rhetorical or comedic purpose, and irony (Choice *C*) is using a word or phrase that expresses the literal opposite of its standard meaning, typically for comedic effect. Thus, Choice *A* is the correct answer.

Blank (ii) is a verb that describes how the work makes viewers feel confusion and horror. Elicit (Choice *E*) means to evoke an emotional reaction. Abates (Choice *D*) denotes a declining intensity, and obviates (Choice *F*) means to avoid or preempt something. Thus, Choice *E* is the correct answer.

7. B, D: Jacob is a terrific team leader, so Blank (i) will be a verb that supports his ability to produce rapid results. Galvanize (Choice *B*) denotes causing a person or group to take sudden action. Enervate (Choice *A*) means to drain someone's mental or physical energy. Venerate (Choice *C*) means to treat with respect. Thus, Choice *B* is the correct answer.

Blank (ii) will describe why Lisa is a poor team leader and possibly relate to how she becomes angry and unapproachable when confronted with a difficult situation. Irascible (Choice *D*) denotes being hotheaded or easily angered. Tortuous (Choice *E*) describes a series of twists and turns, and zealous (Choice *F*) relates to energetically supporting a cause or person. Thus, Choice *D* is the correct answer.

8. B, F, H: The first sentence states that the United States and Scandinavia are different. Blank (i) comes after a clause describing the United States as a multicultural country of immigrants, so the correct answer will be the opposite of multiculturalism. Homogeneous (Choice *B*) denotes something with a universal composition and, in this context, homogenous means monoculture. Ambiguous (Choice *A*) denotes an uncertain meaning, and sedulous (Choice *C*) describes a person who's dedicated or diligent. Thus, Choice *B* is the correct answer.

Blank (ii) will be a noun that "political" can be attached to. Ideology (Choice *F*) is a set of ideas and values that influences one's beliefs. Cacophony (Choice *D*) is a harsh combination of sounds, and hegemony (Choice *E*) denotes dominance over all competitors. Thus, Choice *F* is the correct answer.

Blank (iii) will complement interventionist in describing a foreign policy. Bellicose (Choice *H*) denotes a willingness to enter conflicts. Ambivalent (Choice *G*) refers to having contradictory thoughts about something, and timorous (Choice *I*) means being timid, nervous, or scared. Thus, Choice *H* is the correct answer.

9. A, D, G: The employer pulled the employees aside to prevent a fight from breaking out, so Blank (i) will involve decreasing the tension. Placating (Choice *A*) means to lessen the tension, anger, or hostility. Prevaricating (Choice *B*) means to behave evasively or to hide the truth, and refuting (Choice *C*) denotes proving something is wrong. Refuting is close, but placating more directly relates to dissolving tension and needing to find a workable solution. Thus, Choice *A* is the correct answer.

Blank (ii) is what the employer wants the employees to stop doing to each other. Denigrating (Choice *D*) means attacking someone unfairly or disparagingly. Disabusing (Choice *E*) refers to showing someone why they're wrong, and venerating (Choice *F*) denotes having respect for someone. Thus, Choice *D* is the correct answer.

Blank (iii) is what the employer hopes will happen with the solution. Effectuated (Choice *G*) would mean the solution went into effect. Exculpated (Choice *H*) means proving someone's innocence, and extrapolated (Choice *I*) involves projecting data into the future. Thus, Choice *G* is the correct answer.

10. B, F, G: For **i**, If someone has "uncertainty" pertaining to a subject, the idea is that they are *ambivalent* about the subject, which means they have conflicting emotions about it. Choice *A*, *ebullient*, means enthusiastic, and someone who is "uncertain" about a subject cannot also be *enthusiastic* about it. Choice *C*, *hapless*, means deserving pity, and being uncertain about a president's decision doesn't necessarily call for pity. For **ii**, the best word here is *engaging*, which means participating in something. A war is something that one *engages* in. Choice *D*, *refraining*, is incorrect, because we see that the president *did participate* in the civil war by the end of the sentence, and also one *refrains from* and does not *refrain in* something. Choice *E*, *renounce*, means to abandon or reject, which is the opposite of *engaging in*, and does not make sense by the end of the sentence. For **iii**, the best choice is *impetuous*, because it means acting without thinking. Usually an impetuous decision will cause a "shocked" reaction. Choices *H* and *I*, *temperate* and *impassive*, do not cause "shocked" reactions in people because they mean calm or aloof.

11. A, E: For **i**, *relegated* is the best answer choice because it means to demote to a lower position. The chief was demoted to patrolman. Choices *B* and *C*, *endorsed* and *promoted*, are incorrect, because these imply a raise or an honor of some kind, and we see that the chief was unable to lessen the city's crime rates. For **ii**, *mitigate* means to lessen. Choice *D*, *escalate*, is the opposite of *mitigate*, and the chief wouldn't be demoted because of his inability to *increase* the crime rates. Choice *F*, *transmit*, is also incorrect because this means to spread.

12. B: *Munificent* is the best answer choice here because it means "very generous." The writer had a generous year because she was able to give to charities due to her increase in sales. The word *noxious* means deadly or injurious. The word *inveterate* means long-standing or established. The word *inimical* means not friendly. Finally, *deceptive* means false or wrong. The main implication of the sentence was that she had a prosperous, giving year, and none of the answer choices fit in this context.

13. C, D: For **i**, the best answer choice is *acceded*, which means agree or consent. We see the coworker agreeing to her suggestions because he find out that she *procured*, or won, the account last year, the answer for **ii**. *Admonished* is incorrect because it means to reprimand, and we can see that the coworker admired her. *Swooned* is in the wrong context because it means to faint. For **ii**, *aggregate* means to combine into a collection. While this isn't necessarily wrong, the word *procured* is a better choice because it fits into the entirety of the sentence and its meaning. *Precipitated* means to hurry or speed, so this is incorrect.

14. E: Choice *E*, *rife*, is the best answer choice because it means *abundant*. The island would be *abundant* with turmoil after a hurricane. Choice *A*, sanguine, means optimistic and cheerful; the island would not have been "optimistic with turmoil" after a hurricane, so this is incorrect. Choice *B*, *obdurate*, does have a negative connotation, but it's not the best answer choice because it means stubborn.

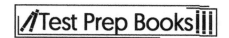

Choice *C*, *mawkish*, means sentimental or emotional, which doesn't fit as well as *rife* in the preposition "with turmoil." Choice *D* means *careful*, and to be *careful with turmoil* doesn't quite fit here, making it incorrect.

15. A, D: The best answer for **i** is *leery*, Choice *A*, because it means suspicious. Since they are camping out at night and there has been a recent bear attack, they would be *suspicious* or *leery* of any noises. For **ii**, the word *cognizant* is the best choice because it means to be aware. The rangers would have to be *aware* or *cognizant* of any threats since they are out patrolling the woods. *Elated* and *assuaged* mean excited and comforted, so these do not fit in with the threatening tone of the sentence. *Oblivious* is an antonym to *cognizant*. *Quarantined* means isolated. The rangers would not be isolated of any threat while on patrol; they would be aware of any threat.

16. C: The correct word here is *premonition* because it means a feeling that something is about to happen. The captain had a feeling about the storm—that it would be worse than the authorities imagined. *Dialect* means local speech, visage means appearance, psyche means personality or inner self, and prestige means influence; none of these words indicates being able to anticipate a violent storm.

Reading Comprehension

17. C: The author contrasts two different viewpoints, then builds a case showing preference for one over the other. Choice *A* is incorrect because the introduction does not contain an impartial definition, but rather another's opinion. Choice *B* is incorrect. There is no puzzling phenomenon given, as the author doesn't mention any peculiar cause or effect that is in question regarding poetry. Choice *D* does contain another's viewpoint at the beginning of the passage; however, to say that the author has no stake in this argument is incorrect; the author uses personal experiences to build their case. Finally, Choice *E* is incorrect because there is no description of the history of poetry offered within the passage.

18. B: Choice *B* accurately describes the author's argument in the text—that poetry is not irrelevant. While the author does praise—and even value—Buddy Wakefield as a poet, he or she never heralds Wakefield as a genius. Eliminate Choice *A*, as it is an exaggeration. Not only is Choice *C* an exaggerated statement, but the author never mentions spoken word poetry in the text. Choice *D* is wrong because this statement contradicts the writer's argument. Choice *E* can also be eliminated, because the author mentions how performance actually *enhances* poetry and that modern technology is one way poetry remains vital.

19. D: *Exiguously* means not occurring often, or occurring rarely, so Choice *D* would LEAST change the meaning of the sentence. Choice *A*, *indolently*, means unhurriedly, or slow, and does not fit the context of the sentence. Choice *B*, *inaudibly*, means quietly or silently. Choice *C*, *interminably*, means endlessly, or all the time, and is the opposite of the word *exiguously*. Choice *E*, *impecunious,* means impoverished or destitute, and does not fit within the context of the sentence.

20. E: The author of the passage tries to insist that performance poetry is a subset of modern poetry, and therefore prove that modern poetry is not "dying," but thriving on social media for the masses. Choice *A* is incorrect, as the author is not refusing any kind of validation. Choice *B* is incorrect; the author's insistence is that poetry will *not* lose popularity. Choice *C* mimics the topic but compares two different genres, while the author makes no comparison in this passage. Choice *D* is incorrect as well; again, there is no cause or effect the author is trying to prove.

21. B: The author's purpose is to disprove Gioia's article claiming that poetry is a dying art form that only survives in academic settings. In order to prove his argument, the author educates the reader about new developments in poetry (Choice *A*) and describes the brilliance of a specific modern poet (Choice *C*), but these are used to serve as examples of a growing poetry trend that counters Gioia's argument. Choice *D* is incorrect because it contradicts the author's argument. Choice *E* is incorrect because the passage uses the performance as a way to convey the author's point; it's not the focus of the piece. It's also unclear if the author was actually present at the live performance.

22. D: This question is difficult because four out of the five choices offer real reasons as to why the author includes the quote. However, the question specifically asks for the *main reason* for including the quote. First off, eliminate Choice *A*. "Speaking meter" doesn't exist and isn't mentioned in the passage. The quote from a recently written poem shows that people are indeed writing, publishing, and performing poetry (Choice *B*). The quote also shows that people are still listening to poetry (Choice *C*). These things are true and, by their nature, serve to disprove Gioia's views (Choice *E*), which is the author's goal. However, Choice *D* is the most direct reason for including the quote, because the article analyzes the quote for its "complex themes" that "draws listeners and appreciation" right after it's given.

23. C: Because the details in Choice *A* and Choice *B* are examples of how an emotionally intelligent leader operates, they are not the best choice for the definition of the term *emotional intelligence*. They are qualities observed in an EI leader. Choice *C* is true as noted in the second sentence of the passage: Emotional Intelligence (EI) includes developing the ability to know one's own emotions, to regulate impulses and emotions, and to use interpersonal communication skills with ease while dealing with other people. It makes sense that someone with well-developed emotional intelligence will have a good handle on understanding his or her emotions and be able to regulate impulses and emotions and use honed interpersonal communication skills. Choice *D* is not a definition of EI. Choice *E* is the opposite of the definition of EI, so both Choice *D* and Choice *E* are incorrect.

24. C: Choice *E* can be eliminated immediately because of the signal word "obviously." Choice *A* can be eliminated because it does not reflect an accurate fact. Choices *B* and *D* do not support claims about how to be a successful leader.

25. E: The qualities of an unsuccessful leader possessing a transactional leadership style are listed in the passage. Choices *A* and *B* are incorrect because these options reflect the qualities of a successful leader. Choices *C* and *D* are definitely not characteristics of a successful leader; however, they are not presented in the passage and readers should do their best to ignore such options.

26. D: Even though some choices may be true of successful leaders, the best answer must be supported by sub-points in the passage. Therefore, Choices *A* and *C* are incorrect. Choice *B* is incorrect because uncompromising transactional leadership styles squelch success. Choice *E* is never mentioned in the passage.

27. A, C, E: After a careful reading of the passage about emotional intelligence, readers can select supporting points for the statements that are true in the selection. For example, the statement that supports Choice *A* says, "Becoming a successful leader in today's industry, government, and nonprofit sectors requires more than a high intelligence quotient (IQ)." Likewise, a supporting passage for Choice *C* is: "Building relationships outside the institution with leadership coaches and with professional development trainers can also help leaders who want to grow their leadership success." To support Choice *E*, the idea that a leader can develop emotional intelligence, if desired, the passage says, "There are ways to develop emotional intelligence for the person who wants to improve his or her leadership style." Choices *B* and *D* do not have supporting evidence in the passage to make them true.

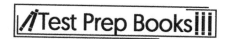

28. D: The use of "I" could serve to have a "hedging" effect, allow the reader to connect with the author in a more personal way, and cause the reader to empathize more with the egrets. However, it doesn't distance the reader from the text, making Choice *D* the answer to this question.

29. C: The quote provides an example of a warden protecting one of the colonies. Choice *A* is incorrect because the speaker of the quote is a warden, not a hunter. Choice *B* is incorrect because the quote does not lighten the mood but shows the danger of the situation between the wardens and the hunters. Choice *D* is incorrect because there is no humor found in the quote.

30. B: An important bird colony. The previous sentence is describing "twenty colonies" of birds, so what follows should be a bird colony. Choice *A* may be true, but we have no evidence of this in the text. Choice *C* does touch on the tension between the hunters and wardens, but there is no official "Bird Island Battle" mentioned in the text. Choice *D* does not exist in the text.

31. D: To demonstrate the success of the protective work of the Audubon Association. The text mentions several different times how and why the association has been successful and gives examples to back this fact. Choice *A* is incorrect because although the article, in some instances, calls certain people to act, it is not the purpose of the entire passage. There is no way to tell if Choices *B* and *C* are correct, as they are not mentioned in the text.

32. C: To have a better opportunity to hunt the birds. Choice *A* might be true in a general sense, but it is not relevant to the context of the text. Choice *B* is incorrect because the hunters are not studying lines of flight to help wardens, but to hunt birds. Choice *D* is incorrect because nothing in the text mentions that hunters are trying to build homes underneath lines of flight of birds for good luck.

33. A: It introduces certain insects that transition from water to air. Choice *B* is incorrect because although the passage talks about gills, it is not the central idea of the passage. Choices *C* and *D* are incorrect because the passage does not "define" or "invite," but only serves as an introduction to stoneflies, dragonflies, and mayflies and their transition from water to air.

34. B: The first paragraph serves as a contrast to the second. Notice how the first paragraph goes into detail describing how insects are able to breathe air. The second paragraph acts as a contrast to the first by stating "[i]t is of great interest to find that, nevertheless, a number of insects spend much of their time under water." Watch for transition words such as "nevertheless" to help find what type of passage you're dealing with.

35. C: The author's tone is informative and exhibits interest in the subject of the study. Overall, the author presents us with information on the subject. One moment where personal interest is depicted is when the author states, "It is of great interest to find that, nevertheless, a number of insects spend much of their time under water."

36. A: The best answer Choice is *A*: the author believes that the stonefly, dragonfly, and mayfly larvae are better prepared to live beneath the water because they have gills that allow them to do so. We see this when the author says "But the larva of a stone-fly, a dragon-fly, or a may-fly is adapted more completely than these for aquatic life; it can, by means of gills of some kind, breathe the air dissolved in water."

37. C: Because a vast majority of insects have wings and also have the ability to breathe underwater. The entire first paragraph talks of how insects have wings, and how insects also have "a system of branching air-tubes" that carries oxygen to the insect's tissues.

38. C, D: The author mentions in the third paragraph how apologia focuses on the short term and reconciliation has long-term goals. In addition, in the second paragraph it describes how reconciliation aims to restore dialogue and apologia seeks to shift blame. Thus, Choices C and D are the correct answers. The first clause in Choice A describes reconciliation rather than apologia, so it's incorrect. Choice B is incorrect because it's never stated or implied that apologia is always delivered in writing. The author doesn't claim that apologia requires actually receiving forgiveness to be effective, and reconciliation involves more than just delivering visual responses, so Choice E is incorrect.

39. E: The author states that national leaders use apologia and reconciliation to restore their image, so it can be inferred that a positive national image is an important part of governance. Thus, Choice E is the correct answer. The author clearly favors reconciliation, but it's unlikely they would agree that national leaders should never apologize. Thus, Choice A is incorrect. Similarly, the author implies that apologia is self-serving but, as described by the author, reconciliation also seems to be self-serving. In any event, the author thinks reconciliation is generally more effective because of its long-term effect, not because it's less self-serving. Thus, Choice B is incorrect. Choices C and D are never mentioned or alluded to in the passage, so they cannot be properly inferred.

40. A, B: Reconciliation's use of symbolic visual images and impact on the long-term relationship between the aggrieved and the transgressor is described in the third paragraph. Thus, Choices A and B are the correct answers. The other answer choices describe features of apologia, not reconciliation, so Choices C, D, and E are all incorrect.

41. E: The author states in the fourth paragraph that offending images don't always require a visual response, but when they do, reconciliation is the better choice due to its long-term goals. Thus, Choice E is the correct answer. Censorship and anti-propaganda campaigns are never mentioned in the passage, so Choices A and B are incorrect. Choices C and D are incorrect because they are directly contradicted in the fourth paragraph.

Sentence Equivalence

42. A, B: Readers may have to draw on their understanding of the Greek word "pur" which means "fire" to come up with the best choices for this sentence equivalence. The immediate match of *bonfires* as a synonym choice then makes sense.

43. B, C: The clue in this sentence is the word "started," which implies that things will become increasingly one way or the other. Looking over the choices, none of the words are similar to "simple," so the best choice is to find synonyms that equal more difficult or clouded meaning, such as *esoteric* and *abstruse*.

44. C, F: Because of the word "legend," the missing word should complete the meaning of the sentence by adding something that means "long lasting." Both the words *ineradicable* and *indelible* suggest leaving a mark forever.

45. B, F: If readers know that the root part of *palatial* means "like a palace," they may see an immediate connection between *palatial* and *extravagant*. Both words fit the meaning of the sentence that suggests the agent is showing places that are not simple and affordable.

46. A, B: Several words work well in this sentence; however, not all words have a synonym partner that would complete the meaning of the sentence except for *malaise* and *angst*. The other words are nouns, but they do not clarify the meaning of the sentence provided.

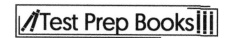

47. A, F: Initially, readers may select a choice that misses the clearest idea of the sentence, just because it works. But remember both synonyms must work to maintain the main idea of the sentence. Two words that do that in this case are *tyro* and *novice*, because they both mean someone who is new at their job.

48. A, B: Notice the signal words "rather than." Look for synonyms that mean something other than a stellar voting record. Note the logic for selecting the first two choices, which insinuate that the senator had past sins that were brought to light. The other choices not only do not have synonyms, but some of them do not complete the full meaning of the sentence.

49. A, F: The key word in the passage is "thick." Even if readers have not seen the commercial, they can visualize the slow motion of a pearl dropped into a bottle of thick shampoo. Choices *B, C, D,* and *E* do not suggest a relationship to slow movement. Although *viscous* and *gradual* are not synonyms, they both indicate properties that have a thick, or slow, movement.

50. B, E: Readers might recognize that the tone of the sentence is negative and short, as the writer used the word "abrupt." The two synonyms that best complete the meaning of the sentence are *laconic* and *terse*, which reflect a player's annoyance with the post-game media interview process.

GRE Verbal Practice Test #3

Text Completion

Select the best word from the corresponding column of choices that most clearly completes the passage:

1. The law student immediately recognized the (i) _____ argumentation on the exam and set the question right. Those (ii) _____ years in law school had finally paid off.

Blank (i)	Blank (ii)
a. palatable	d. vivacious
b. capricious	e. arduous
c. fallacious	f. lackadaisical

2. The actor's (i) _____ of famous actors such as Marlon Brando and Al Pacino made him the life of the party.

Blank (i)
a. empathy
b. anecdotes
c. hypothesis
d. jubilation
e. vindication

3. The old woman's (i) _____ made her a pillar of her community and everyone's (ii) _____ way of obtaining advice.

Blank (i)	Blank (ii)
a. enmity	d. myopic
b. sagacity	e. preferred
c. impetuosity	f. variegated

4. We wanted to (i) _____ the flavor of the watermelon, so we added salt to it.

Blank (i)
a. enhance
b. discount
c. disdain
d. abbreviate
e. suppress

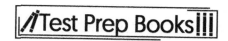

5. The athlete displayed remarkable (i) _____ after her injury. In fact, during her (ii) _____, the doctor told her that she was the most (iii) _____ patient he had ever seen.

Blank (i)	Blank (ii)	Blank (iii)
a. prosperity	d. expedition	g. befuddled
b. opulence	e. bereavement	h. deranged
c. resilience	f. convalescence	i. tenacious

6. After the huge disagreement we had the night before, we agreed to settle on a (i) _____ in order to keep the peace.

Blank (i)
a. altercation
b. prescription
c. fetter
d. compromise
e. pyre

7. The South American dictator was considered a (i) _____ who tormented his citizens and created unprecedented (ii) _____ in the surrounding areas.

Blank (i)	Blank (ii)
a. despot	d. exorbitance
b. novice	e. adversity
c. martyr	f. affluence

8. It was apparent that King Louis XVI and the Queen consort Marie Antoinette, with their lavish wardrobes and sprawling estates, led a (i) _____ lifestyle that ultimately contributed to their demise.

Blank (i)
a. meticulous
b. intrepid
c. bombastic
d. stalwart
e. enterprising

9. The character was a quintessential Jungian (i) _____ that displayed traits of the hero, journeyed into the enemy's territory, and defeated the villain.

Blank (i)
a. orator
b. rhetorician
c. connoisseur
d. authority
e. archetype

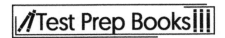

10. The judge showed his (i) _____ toward the woman when he dismissed her case altogether and ruled a(n) (ii) _____ .

Blank (i)	Blank (ii)
a. idiosyncrasy	d. acquittal
b. parcel	e. prohibition
c. bias	f. exclusion

11. They were able to (i) _____ his name after a DNA test proved that he was not at the crime scene.

Blank (i)
a. vindicate
b. suppress
c. impute
d. emulate
e. censure

12. The scientists' (i) _____ (ii) was that the emissions coming from the Volkwagen Diesel engines from 2008 to 2015 were _____ to the environment.

Blank (i)	Blank (ii)
a. hypothesis	d. vigorous
b. promiscuity	e. amalgamated
c. proportion	f. deleterious

13. Becoming a doctor was (i) _____ since her childhood; she loved working with people and wanted to help others recover as quickly as possible.

Blank (i)
a. dubious
b. futile
c. calamitous
d. inevitable
e. mandatory

14. Later that evening, he went home and lied (i) _____ in bed, unable to sleep, still thinking about the (ii) _____ events that day.

Blank (i)	Blank (ii)
a. restlessly	d. insipid
b. soundly	e. vexing
c. tacitly	f. auspicious

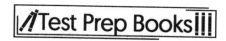

15. The social worker had (i) _____ concern that the client might not have the (ii) _____ to follow through and achieve their personal goals.

Blank (i)	Blank (ii)
a. astute	d. resolution
b. untenable	e. sagacity
c. justifiable	f. intuition

16. The nurse had studied ceaselessly and trained his focus for the past months, so he was (i) _____ during the exam, confident that he would ace the recertification.

Blank (i)
a. anxious
b. vacant
c. impulsive
d. imperturbable
e. rash

Reading Comprehension

Questions 17–21 are based upon the following passage:

"Did you ever come across a protégé of his—one Hyde?" He asked.

"Hyde?" repeated Lanyon. "No. Never heard of him. Since my time."

That was the amount of information that the lawyer carried back with him to the great, dark bed on which he tossed to and fro until the small hours of the morning began to grow large. It was a night of little ease to his toiling mind, toiling in mere darkness and besieged by questions.

Six o'clock struck on the bells of the church that was so conveniently near to Mr. Utterson's dwelling, and still he was digging at the problem. Hitherto it had touched him on the intellectual side alone; but now his imagination also was engaged, or rather enslaved; and as he lay and tossed in the gross darkness of the night in the curtained room, Mr. Enfield's tale went by before his mind in a scroll of lighted pictures. He would be aware of the great field of lamps in a nocturnal city; then of the figure of a man walking swiftly; then of a child running from the doctor's; and then these met, and that human Juggernaut trod the child down and passed on regardless of her screams. Or else he would see a room in a rich house, where his friend lay asleep, dreaming and smiling at his dreams; and then the door of that room would be opened, the curtains of the bed plucked apart, the sleeper recalled, and, lo! There would stand by his side a figure to whom power was given, and even at that dead hour he must rise and do its bidding. The figure in these two phrases haunted the lawyer all night; and if at anytime he dozed over, it was but to see it glide more stealthily through sleeping houses, or move the more swiftly, and still the more smoothly, even to dizziness, through wider labyrinths of lamplighted city, and at every street corner crush a child and leave her screaming. And still the figure had no face by which he might know it; even in his dreams it had no face, or one that baffled him and melted before his eyes; and thus there it was that there sprung up and grew apace in the lawyer's mind a singularly strong, almost an inordinate, curiosity to behold the features of the real Mr. Hyde. If he could but once set eyes on him, he thought the mystery would lighten and perhaps roll altogether away, as was the habit of mysterious things when well examined. He might see a reason for his friend's strange preference or bondage, and even for the startling clauses of the will. And at least it would be a face worth seeing: the face of a man who was without bowels of mercy: a face which had but to show itself to raise up, in the mind of the unimpressionable Enfield, a spirit of enduring hatred.

From that time forward, Mr. Utterson began to haunt the door in the by-street of shops. In the morning before office hours, at noon when business was plenty and time scarce, at night under the face of the full city moon, by all lights and at all hours of solitude or concourse, the lawyer was to be found on his chosen post.

"If he be Mr. Hyde," he had thought, "I should be Mr. Seek."

Excerpt from *The Strange Case of Dr. Jekyll and Mr. Hyde* by Robert Louis Stevenson

Select only one answer choice:

17. What is the purpose of the use of repetition in the following passage?

It was a night of little ease to his toiling mind, toiling in mere darkness and besieged by questions.

a. It serves as a demonstration of the mental state of Mr. Lanyon.
b. It is reminiscent of the church bells that are mentioned in the story.
c. It mimics Mr. Utterson's ambivalence.
d. It emphasizes Mr. Utterson's anguish in failing to identify Hyde's whereabouts.

Select only one answer choice:

18. What is the setting of the story in this passage?
a. In the city
b. On the countryside
c. In a jail
d. In a mental health facility

Select only one answer choice:

19. The phrase *labyrinths of lamplighted city* contains an example of what?
a. Hyperbole
b. Simile
c. Juxtaposition
d. Alliteration

Select only one answer choice:

20. What can one reasonably conclude from the final comment of this passage?

   "If he be Mr. Hyde," he had thought, "I should be Mr. Seek."

   a. The speaker is considering a name change.
   b. The speaker is experiencing an identity crisis.
   c. The speaker has mistakenly been looking for the wrong person.
   d. The speaker intends to continue to look for Hyde.

Select only one answer choice:

21. According to the passage, what is Mr. Utterson struggling with as he tosses and turns in bed?
   a. A murderer who is stalking Mr. Utterson since he moved to the city.
   b. The mystery surrounding a dark figure and the terrible crimes he commits.
   c. The cases he is involved in as a detective.
   d. A chronic illness that is causing Mr. Utterson to hallucinate.

Questions 22–28 are based on the following passage.

In the quest to understand existence, modern philosophers must question if humans can fully comprehend the world. Classical western approaches to philosophy tend to hold that one can understand something, be it an event or object, by standing outside of the phenomena and observing it. It is then by unbiased observation that one can grasp the details of the world. This seems to hold true for many things. Scientists conduct experiments and record their findings, and thus many natural phenomena become comprehendible. However, several of these observations were possible because humans used tools in order to make these discoveries.

This may seem like an extraneous matter. After all, people invented things like microscopes and telescopes in order to enhance their capacity to view cells or the movement of stars. While humans are still capable of seeing things, the question remains if human beings have the capacity to fully observe and see the world in order to understand it. It would not be an impossible stretch to argue that what humans see through a microscope is not the exact thing itself, but a human interpretation of it.

This would seem to be the case in the "Business of the Holes" experiment conducted by Richard Feynman. To study the way electrons behave, Feynman set up a barrier with two holes and a plate. The plate was there to indicate how many times the electrons would pass through the hole(s). Rather than casually observe the electrons acting under normal circumstances, Feynman discovered that electrons behave in two totally different ways depending on whether or not they are observed. The electrons that were observed had passed through either one of the holes or were caught on the plate as particles. However, electrons that weren't observed acted as waves instead of particles and passed through both holes. This indicated that electrons have a dual nature. Electrons seen by the human eye act like particles, while unseen electrons act like waves of energy.

This dual nature of the electrons presents a conundrum. While humans now have a better understanding of electrons, the fact remains that people cannot entirely perceive how electrons behave without the use of instruments. We can only observe one of the mentioned behaviors, which only provides a partial understanding of the entire function of electrons. Therefore, we're forced to ask ourselves whether the world we observe is objective or if it is subjectively perceived by humans. Or, an alternative question: can man understand the world only through machines that will allow them to observe natural phenomena?

Both questions humble man's capacity to grasp the world. However, those ideas don't take into account that many phenomena have been proven by human beings without the use of machines, such as the discovery of gravity. Like all philosophical questions, whether man's reason and observation alone can understand the universe can be approached from many angles.

Consider each of the choices separately and select all that apply:

22. The word *extraneous* in paragraph two can be best interpreted as referring to which of the following?
    a. Indispensable
    b. Bewildering
    c. Expendable
    d. Exuberant
    e. Superfluous

Select only one answer choice:

23. What is the author's motivation for writing the passage?
    a. To bring to light an alternative view on human perception by examining the role of technology in human understanding.
    b. To educate the reader on the latest astroparticle physics discovery and offer terms that may be unfamiliar to the reader.
    c. To argue that humans are totally blind to the realities of the world by presenting an experiment that proves that electrons are not what they seem on the surface.
    d. To reflect on opposing views of human understanding.
    e. To disprove classical philosophy by comparing more accurate technology to the speculations of the ancient philosophers.

Select only one answer choice:

24. Which of the following most closely resembles the way in which paragraph four is structured?
    a. It offers one solution, questions the solution, and then ends with an alternative solution.
    b. It presents an inquiry, explains the detail of that inquiry, and then offers a solution.
    c. It presents a problem, explains the details of that problem, and then ends with more inquiry.
    d. It gives a definition, offers an explanation, and then ends with an inquiry.
    e. It presents a problem, offers an example, and then ends with a solution.

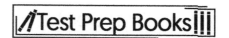

Select only one answer choice:

25. For the classical approach to understanding to hold true, which of the following must be required?
    a. A telescope.
    b. A recording device.
    c. Multiple witnesses present.
    d. The person observing must be unbiased.
    e. The person observing must prove their theory beyond a doubt.

Select only one answer choice:

26. Which best describes how the electrons in the experiment behaved like waves?
    a. The electrons moved up and down like actual waves.
    b. The electrons passed through both holes and then onto the plate.
    c. The electrons converted to photons upon touching the plate.
    d. The electrons were seen passing through one hole or the other.
    e. The electrons were glowing during the experiment, indicating light waves were moving them.

Select only one answer choice:

27. The author mentions "gravity" in the last paragraph in order to do what?
    a. In order to show that different natural phenomena test man's ability to grasp the world.
    b. To prove that since man has not measured it with the use of tools or machines, humans cannot know the true nature of gravity.
    c. To demonstrate an example of natural phenomena humans discovered and understood without the use of tools or machines.
    d. To show an alternative solution to the nature of electrons that humans have not thought of yet.
    e. To look toward the future of technology so that we may understand the dual nature of all phenomena, including gravity.

Select only one answer choice:

28. Which situation best parallels the revelation of the dual nature of electrons discovered in Feynman's experiment?
a. Ancient Greeks believed that Zeus hurled lightning down to Earth. In reality, lightning is caused by supercharged electrons, and happens either inside the clouds or between the cloud and the ground.
b. The coelacanth was thought to be extinct, but a live specimen was just recently discovered. There are now two living species of coelacanth known to man, and both are believed to be endangered.
c. In the Middle Ages, blacksmiths added carbon to iron, thus inventing steel. The consequences of this important discovery would have its biggest effects during the industrial revolution.
d. In order to better examine and treat broken bones, the x-ray machine was invented and put to use in hospitals and medical centers.
e. A man is born color-blind and grows up observing everything in lighter or darker shades. With the invention of special goggles he puts on, he discovers that there are other colors in addition to different shades.

Questions 29–31 are based on the following passage:

Despite spending far more on health care than any other nation, the United States ranks near the bottom on key health indicators. This paradox has been attributed to underinvestment in addressing social and behavioral determinants of health. A recent Institute of Medicine (IOM) report linked the shorter overall life expectancy in the United States to problems that are either caused by behavioral risks (e.g., injuries and homicides, adolescent pregnancy and sexually transmitted infections (STIs), HIV/AIDS, drug-related deaths, lung diseases, obesity, and diabetes) or affected by social conditions (e.g., birth outcomes, heart disease, and disability).

While spending more than other countries per capita on health care services, the United States spends less on average than do other nations on social services impacting social and behavioral determinants of health. Bradley, et al., found that Organization for Economic Co-operation and Development (OECD) nations with a higher ratio of spending on social services relative to health care services have better health and longer life expectancies than do those like the United States that have a lower ratio.

The Clinical & Translational Science Awards (CTSAs) established by the National Institutes of Health (NIH) have helped initiate interdisciplinary programs in more than sixty institutions that aim to advance the translation of research findings from "bench" to "bedside" to "community." Social and behavioral issues are inherent aspects of the translation of findings at the bench into better care and better health. Insofar as Clinical and Translational Science Institutes (CTSIs) will be evaluated for renewal—not only on the basis of their bench science discoveries, but also by their ability to move these discoveries into practice and improve individual and population health—the CTSIs should be motivated to include social and behavioral scientists in their work.

Population Health: Behavioral and Social Science Insights, Robert M. Kaplan et al. (2015), published by the Agency for Healthcare Research and Quality (National Institutes of Health), "Determinants of Health and Longevity" by Nancy E. Adler and Aric A. Prather, excerpted from pages 411 and 417

Consider each of the choices separately and select all that apply:

29. Which statement(s) describes how the United States differs in its approach to health care compared with other nations?
    a. On average, the United States spends less on social services impacting social and behavioral determinants of health than other nations.
    b. Compared with other nations, the United States has a higher ratio of spending on social services relative to health care services.
    c. Compared with other nations, the United States spends more per capita on health care services despite producing worse health outcomes.
    d. Compared with other nations, the United States has a lower life expectancy due to its lack of spending on health care services.
    e. Unlike other nations, the United States doesn't fund interdisciplinary programs that include behavioral and social science.

Select only one answer choice:

30. Based on the passage, which statement(s) describes the primary purpose of the Clinical and Translational Science Awards?
    a. The Clinical and Translational Science Awards advocate for the expansion of social services in the United States.
    b. The Clinical and Translational Science Awards seek to advance the translation of research findings from "bench" to "bedside" to "community."
    c. The Clinical and Translational Science Awards conduct research on how to mitigate the behavioral risks that have caused the decline in Americans' life expectancy.
    d. The Clinical and Translational Science Awards exclusively employ social and behavioral scientists, filling a void in the American health care system.
    e. The Clinical and Translational Science Awards calculate the optimal ratio for spending on social services relative to health care services.

Select only one answer choice:

31. Which statement(s) most accurately identifies the author's main thesis?
    a. Despite outspending other countries on health care, the United States performs poorly on key health indicators.
    b. The National Institutes of Health created the Clinical and Translational Science Awards to develop interdisciplinary programs in more than sixty institutions.
    c. Social and behavioral factors are an underappreciated aspect of health, and if they are better understood and properly addressed, health outcomes will improve.
    d. The United States has the shortest overall life expectancy in the world due to unaddressed behavioral risks and deteriorating social conditions.
    e. Life expectancy is the most important health care indicator because it encapsulates every other relevant factor.

Questions 32–36 are based on the following passage.

"MANKIND being originally equals in the order of creation, the equality could only be destroyed by some subsequent circumstance; the distinctions of rich, and poor, may in a great measure be accounted for, and that without having recourse to the harsh ill sounding names of oppression and avarice. Oppression is often the consequence, but seldom or never the means of riches; and though avarice will preserve a man from being necessitously poor, it generally makes him too timorous to be wealthy.

But there is another and greater distinction for which no truly natural or religious reason can be assigned, and that is, the distinction of men into KINGS and SUBJECTS. Male and female are the distinctions of nature, good and bad the distinctions of heaven; but how a race of men came into the world so exalted above the rest, and distinguished like some new species, is worth enquiring into, and whether they are the means of happiness or of misery to mankind.

In the early ages of the world, according to the scripture chronology, there were no kings; the consequence of which was there were no wars; it is the pride of kings which throw mankind into confusion. Holland without a king hath enjoyed more peace for this last century than any of the monarchical governments in Europe. Antiquity favors the same remark; for the quiet and rural lives of the first patriarchs hath a happy something in them, which vanishes away when we come to the history of Jewish royalty.

Government by kings was first introduced into the world by the Heathens, from whom the children of Israel copied the custom. It was the most prosperous invention the Devil ever set on foot for the promotion of idolatry. The Heathens paid divine honors to their deceased kings, and the Christian world hath improved on the plan by doing the same to their living ones. How impious is the title of sacred majesty applied to a worm, who in the midst of his splendor is crumbling into dust!

As the exalting one man so greatly above the rest cannot be justified on the equal rights of nature, so neither can it be defended on the authority of scripture; for the will of the Almighty, as declared by Gideon and the prophet Samuel, expressly disapproves of government by kings. All anti-monarchical parts of scripture have been very smoothly glossed over in monarchical governments, but they undoubtedly merit the attention of countries, which have their governments yet to form. "Render unto Caesar the things which are Caesar's" is the scripture doctrine of courts, yet it is no support of monarchical government, for the Jews at that time were without a king, and in a state of vassalage to the Romans.

Near three thousand years passed away from the Mosaic account of the creation, till the Jews under a national delusion requested a king. Till then their form of government (except in extraordinary cases, where the Almighty interposed) was a kind of republic administered by a judge and the elders of the tribes. Kings they had none, and it was held sinful to acknowledge any being under that title but the Lord of Hosts. And when a man seriously reflects on the idolatrous homage which is paid to the persons of Kings, he need not wonder, that the Almighty ever jealous of his honor, should disapprove of a form of government which so impiously invades the prerogative of heaven.

Excerpt From: Thomas Paine. "Common Sense."

32. According to passage, what role does avarice, or greed, play in poverty?
    a. It can make a man very wealthy.
    b. It is the consequence of wealth.
    c. Avarice can prevent a man from being poor, but too fearful to be very wealthy.
    d. Avarice is what drives a person to be very wealthy

33. Of these distinctions, which does the author believe to be beyond natural or religious reason?
    a. Good and bad
    b. Male and female
    c. Human and animal
    d. King and subjects

34. According to the passage, what are the Heathens responsible for?
    a. Government by kings
    b. Quiet and rural lives of patriarchs
    c. Paying divine honors to their living kings
    d. Equal rights of nature

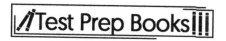

35. Which of the following best states Paine's rationale for the denouncement of monarchy?
    a. It is against the laws of nature.
    b. It is against the equal rights of nature and is denounced in scripture.
    c. Despite scripture, a monarchal government is unlawful.
    d. Neither the law nor scripture denounce monarchy.

36. Based on the passage, what is the best definition of the word *idolatrous*?
    a. Worshipping heroes
    b. Being deceitful
    c. Sinfulness
    d. Engaging in illegal activities

Questions 37–41 are based on the following passage:

As long ago as 1860 it was the proper thing to be born at home. At present, so I am told, the high gods of medicine have decreed that the first cries of the young shall be uttered upon the anesthetic air of a hospital, preferably a fashionable one. So young Mr. and Mrs. Roger Button were fifty years ahead of style when they decided, one day in the summer of 1860, that their first baby should be born in a hospital. Whether this anachronism had any bearing upon the astonishing history I am about to set down will never be known.

I shall tell you what occurred, and let you judge for yourself.

The Roger Buttons held an enviable position, both social and financial, in ante-bellum Baltimore. They were related to the This Family and the That Family, which, as every Southerner knew, entitled them to membership in that enormous peerage which largely populated the Confederacy. This was their first experience with the charming old custom of having babies— Mr. Button was naturally nervous. He hoped it would be a boy so that he could be sent to Yale College in Connecticut, at which institution Mr. Button himself had been known for four years by the somewhat obvious nickname of "Cuff."

On the September morning <u>consecrated</u> to the enormous event he arose nervously at six o'clock, dressed himself, adjusted an impeccable stock, and hurried forth through the streets of Baltimore to the hospital, to determine whether the darkness of the night had borne in new life upon its bosom.

When he was approximately a hundred yards from the Maryland Private Hospital for Ladies and Gentlemen he saw Doctor Keene, the family physician, descending the front steps, rubbing his hands together with a washing movement—as all doctors are required to do by the unwritten ethics of their profession.

Mr. Roger Button, the president of Roger Button & Co., Wholesale Hardware, began to run toward Doctor Keene with much less dignity than was expected from a Southern gentleman of that picturesque period. "Doctor Keene!" he called. "Oh, Doctor Keene!"

The doctor heard him, faced around, and stood waiting, a curious expression settling on his harsh, medicinal face as Mr. Button drew near.

"What happened?" demanded Mr. Button, as he came up in a gasping rush. "What was it? How is she? A boy? Who is it? What—"

"Talk sense!" said Doctor Keene sharply. He appeared somewhat irritated.

"Is the child born?" begged Mr. Button.

Doctor Keene frowned. "Why, yes, I suppose so—after a fashion." Again he threw a curious glance at Mr. Button.

From *The Curious Case of Benjamin Button* by F.S. Fitzgerald, 1922.

Select only one answer choice:

37. According to the passage, what major event is about to happen in this story?
    a. Mr. Button is about to go to a funeral.
    b. Mr. Button's wife is about to have a baby.
    c. Mr. Button is getting ready to go to the doctor's office.
    d. Mr. Button is about to go shopping for new clothes.

Select only one answer choice:

38. What kind of tone does the above passage have?
    a. Nervous and Excited
    b. Sad and Angry
    c. Shameful and Confused
    d. Grateful and Joyous

Select only one answer choice:

39. Which of the following best describes the development of this passage?
    a. It starts in the middle of a narrative in order to transition smoothly to a conclusion.
    b. It is a chronological narrative from beginning to end.
    c. The sequence of events is backwards—we go from future events to past events.
    d. To introduce the setting of the story and its characters.

Select only one answer choice:

40. The main purpose of the first paragraph is:
    a. To explain the setting of the narrative and give information about the story.
    b. To present the thesis so that the audience can determine which points are valid later in the text.
    c. To introduce a counterargument so that the author can refute it in the next paragraph.
    d. To provide a description of the speaker's city and the building in which he works.

Select only one answer choice:

41. The end of the passage implies to the audience that:
    a. There is bad weather coming.
    b. The doctor thinks Mr. Button is annoying.
    c. The baby and the mother did not make it through labor.
    d. Something is unusual about the birth of the baby.

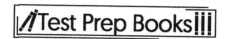

Sentence Equivalence (9)

Select the two answer choices that can complete the sentence and create sentences that have complementary meaning.

42. The starving man was disheartened when he reached the summit of the hill and realized that only a(n) _____ wasteland awaited him.
    a. fruitful
    b. infertile
    c. sumptuous
    d. lavish
    e. barren
    f. feracious

43. The rebels fought in order to _____ their brothers from the evil dictator.
    a. agitate
    b. instigate
    c. liberate
    d. release
    e. fracture
    f. plague

44. When the baseball game was over, the first thing Jackson did was run towards the dugout to grab his water bottle to relieve his _____ throat.
    a. humid
    b. scorched
    c. parched
    d. dusty
    e. dissonant
    f. arid

45. Driving across the United States, the two friends became more _____ each time they arrived in a new state. They shared many good memories on that trip they would remember for the rest of their lives.
    a. attached
    b. distant
    c. suffering
    d. irritable
    e. inseparable
    f. mellow

46. After Kira wrote her first book, she _____ her fans the sequel would be just as exciting as the first.
    a. guaranteed
    b. promised
    c. invigorated
    d. germinated
    e. denied
    f. warned

47. When I heard the wolf howl from my tent, my hands started _____ and my heart stopped . . . hopefully I would make it through this night alive!
    a. dancing
    b. glowing
    c. shaking
    d. throbbing
    e. trembling
    f. pulsating

48. The bullies _____ the younger boy, causing him to feel worthless.
    a. despaired
    b. belittled
    c. broke
    d. disparaged
    e. sparred
    f. endorsed

49. As soon as the shot rang out, the runners _____ toward the finish line.
    a. sprinted
    b. skipped
    c. dashed
    d. herded
    e. rejoiced
    f. amassed

50. When she saw the crayon drawings on the wall, the mother had no choice but to _____ her sons.
    a. honor
    b. chastise
    c. choose
    d. stagnate
    e. locate
    f. rebuke

Answer Explanations #3

Text Completion

1. C, E: *Fallacious* means based on incorrect reasoning. To set a question right, the student would have to be confronted with *false* or *fallacious* reasoning on the exam. *Palatable* means delicious or agreeable, and we don't normally talk about argumentation as being either of these things. *Capricious* means a sudden behavior change and is used to describe people, not argumentation. For **ii**, *arduous* is the best choice because it means difficult. Usually if we see that something "pays off" in the end, it means that it was difficult to endure. *Vivacious* means lively or spirited, so this would not be used to describe years in law school. Neither would the word *lackadaisical*, which means careless or indifferent.

2. B: The correct answer here is *anecdotes*, Choice *B*, because it means a short account of an event or events, or a story. The actor telling stories about other famous actors would make him the life of the party. *Empathy* means to share feelings with another; this word doesn't fit here because the actor empathizing with celebrities wouldn't necessarily make him popular at a party. The same goes with the words hypothesis (theory requiring proof), jubilation (joy), and vindication (to clear from blame).

3. B, E: For **i**, the best answer choice is *sagacity*, because it means wisdom. Wisdom would make one a pillar of one's community as well as an advice-giver. *Enmity* means hatred, so this would not make her a pillar of the community, and neither would *impetuosity*, which means rashness. For **ii**, *preferred* is the best answer choice because it means favorite or chosen. It was their *favorite* way of obtaining advice. *Myopic* means nearsighted, so this isn't the right word to used for a way of obtaining advice. Neither is *variegated*, which means diversified.

4. A: *Enhance* is the best answer choice here because it means to improve. They want to *improve* or *boost* the flavor of the watermelon by adding salt to it. *Discount* is incorrect because it usually pertains to sales economy, not taste. *Disdain* means to regard with scorn, which doesn't quite fit the context here. *Abbreviate* means to shorten and is usually used in context with shortening words, not flavor. *Suppress* means to restrain; one wouldn't try to *suppress* flavor with salt. Salt tends to enhance the flavor of food.

5. C, F, I: For **i**, we would say that the athlete displayed remarkable *resilience* after her injury, because resilience means the ability to recover quickly. *Prosperity* (wealth) and *opulence* (affluence) aren't usually things someone would display after an injury. For **ii**, *convalescence* is the best answer choice here because it means the gradual period of returning back to health. *Bereavement* means a period of grief or mourning, so this is incorrect. *Expedition* is also incorrect because it means a group of people going on a journey. For **iii**, *tenacious* is the best answer choice because it means strong or unyielding. She would be a *strong* patient due to her fast recovery. *Deranged* means mentally ill or insane, so this does not fit in with the context of recovering from a sports injury. *Befuddled* means confused, so this is also not appropriate here because there is no indication in the sentence that the patient is confused.

6. D: The best answer choice here is *D*, *compromise*, which means to settle differences. *Altercation* is incorrect because it means a fight, and two people wouldn't settle a fight with a fight. *Prescription* means formula or medicine, and this also doesn't make sense in settling a disagreement. *Fetter* means shackle, so this does not fit into the context. *Pyre* means a heap of wood, and like the others, one wouldn't use a heap of wood to settle an argument.

7. A, E: For **i**, *despot* is the best answer choice because it means a cruel and oppressive dictator. The term *novice* means someone who is new at something, and someone who is new or a beginner at leadership would probably not have enough experience to be considered a dictator. *Martyr* is also incorrect; this word often denotes a saint of some sort who suffers or dies in order to stand up for something they believe in. This does not fit in the context of a leader who torments his citizens. For **ii**, the best word is *adversity* because it means bad fortune or circumstance. The words *exorbitance* and *affluence* have to do with wealth, so these are incorrect.

8. C: The best word here is *bombastic*, which means an inflated display of wealth. *Meticulous* means detailed, which isn't specific enough to describe the type of lifestyle being displayed. *Intrepid* and *stalwart* mean brave or strong, so these also don't fit the royal lifestyle. *Enterprising* means resourceful or energetic, and lavish wardrobes and sprawling estates are the opposite of displaying resourcefulness.

9. E: The word *archetype* means a model or pattern used over and over again to demonstrate a type of character or situation. A hero is a common archetype used in narratives. *Orator* and *rhetorician* both denote a speaker of some kind. *Connoisseur* and *authority* both mean a master or specialist of some sort and do not display a pattern of characterization like the word *archetype* does.

10. C, D: For **i**, *bias* is the best word to use here because it means partiality; in this sentence, the judge favors the woman and shows favoritism toward her case. *Idiosyncrasy* is incorrect because it means oddity, and that doesn't apply to the context here. *Parcel* does not make sense here because it describes a container to hold something in. For **ii**, *acquittal* is when the judge finds the evidence insufficient to make a conviction. *Prohibition* and *exclusion* both mean a forbiddance to something, and we see that the judge dismissed her case, so these do not fit here.

11. A: *Vindicate* is the best word here because it means to clear from blame. They were able to clear his name from blame after finding out he was not at the crime scene. *Suppress* means to stifle or end something, *impute* means attribute, *emulate* means to copy the actions of, and *censure* means severe criticism or stifling of something, so these are not the best answer choices for something that is meant to clear someone's name or erase their past convictions.

12. A, F: For **i**, the best answer choice is *hypothesis*, which means theory or conclusion. *Promiscuity* means lewdness and *proportion* means relative amount of something, so these do not make sense when discussing scientific conclusions. For **ii**, the best word choice is *deleterious*, which means harmful. The other two word choices, *vigorous* (energetic) and *amalgamated* (blended) do not describe emission effects in the environment.

13. D: *Inevitable* is the best choice here because it means unavoidable or certain. It was unavoidable that she would become a doctor since she demonstrated all the characteristics that good doctors possess. The other word choices describe an unlucky or forced event, and since we see that she liked to help people and wanted others to recover, we would want to pick a word that has a positive connotation, such as *inevitable*.

14. A, E: For **i**, the best choice is *restlessly*, because the sentence goes on to say he was unable to sleep. *Soundly* would mean he slept peacefully, while *tacitly* is a word meaning something is already understood. For **ii**, the *vexing*, causing concern or worry, is the best choice. In this context, *insipid* could mean uninteresting, but then there's no reason for them to keep him awake. *Auspicious* is close but not quite a good fit for the sentence, meaning something is favorable or a sign of success.

15. C, D: For **i**, the best word is *justifiable*, meaning with provable reason or good cause. *Astute* means intelligent or clever, and thus does not describe a reason for concern. *Untenable* could fit into the context, but it also doesn't provide a reason for concern, because it's an antonym of *justifiable*, and would mean the social worker's concern was unfounded. For **ii**, the best choice is *resolution*, in this context referring to the client's willpower or determination to achieve their goals. The other choices, *sagacity* and *intuition*, are not the best option, since the client's intelligence or foresight are less important to following through on their goals.

16. D: *Imperturbable* is the best word for this sentence, meaning the nurse was composed or calm, which aligns with the studying and training he did, and his confidence he'd get recertified. *Anxious* means uneasy or worried. *Vacant* in this sentence could mean being absentminded or expressionless, but that's not the best fit with his focus and confidence. *Impulsive* and *rash* both refer to acting without forethought or planning, or reckless behavior, so they contradict the rest of the sentence.

Reading Comprehension

17. D: It emphasizes Mr. Utterson's anguish in failing to identify Hyde's whereabouts. Context clues indicate that Choice *D* is correct because the passage provides great detail of Mr. Utterson's feelings about locating Hyde. Choice *A* does not fit because there is no mention of Mr. Lanyon's mental state. Choice *B* is incorrect; although the text does make mention of bells, Choice *B* is not the *best* answer overall. Choice *C* is incorrect because the passage clearly states that Mr. Utterson was determined, not unsure.

18. A: In the city. The word *city* appears in the passage several times, thus establishing the location for the reader.

19. D: This is an example of alliteration. Choice *D* is the correct answer because of the repetition of the *L*-words. Hyperbole is an exaggeration, so Choice *A* doesn't work. No comparison is being made, so no simile or juxtaposition is being used, thus eliminating Choices *B* and *C*.

20. D: The speaker intends to continue to look for Hyde. Choices *A* and *B* are not possible answers because the text doesn't refer to any name changes or an identity crisis, despite Mr. Utterson's extreme obsession with finding Hyde. The text also makes no mention of a mistaken identity when referring to Hyde, so Choice *C* is also incorrect.

21. B: Mr. Utterson is struggling with the mystery surrounding a dark figure and the terrible crimes he commits. As Mr. Utterson tosses and turns in bed in the long paragraph, we see him wanting to discern the figure's face as he imagines him committing the crimes, but Mr. Utterson has no idea who the figure is.

22. C, E: *Extraneous* most nearly means *superfluous* or *expendable*, which means trivial or unnecessary. Choice *A, indispensable,* is incorrect because it means the opposite of *extraneous*. Choice *B, bewildering,* means *confusing* and is not relevant to the context of the sentence. Finally, Choice *D* is incorrect because although the prefix of the word is the same, *ex-*, the word *exuberant* means *elated* or *enthusiastic*, and is irrelevant to the context of the sentence.

23. A: This is a challenging question because the author's purpose is somewhat open-ended. The author concludes by stating that the questions regarding human perception and observation can be approached from many angles. Thus, the author does not seem to be attempting to prove one thing or another. Choice *B* is incorrect because we cannot know for certain whether the electron experiment is the latest discovery in astroparticle physics because no date is given. Choice *C* is a broad generalization that does not reflect accurately on the writer's views. While the author does appear to reflect on opposing views of human understanding (Choice *D*), the best answer is Choice *A*. Choice *E* is also wrong because the author never says that classical philosophy is wrong or directly attempts to debunk it.

24. C: It presents a problem, explains the details of that problem, and then ends with more inquiry. The beginning of this paragraph literally "presents a conundrum," explains the problem of partial understanding, and then ends with more questions, or inquiry. There is no solution offered in this paragraph, making Choices *A, B,* and *E* incorrect. Choice *D* is incorrect because the paragraph does not begin with a definition.

25. D: Looking back in the text, the author describes that classical philosophy holds that understanding can be reached by careful observation. This will not work if they are overly invested or biased in their pursuit. Choices *A, B,* and *C* are in no way related and are completely unnecessary. A specific theory is not necessary to understanding, according to classical philosophy mentioned by the author. Again, the key to understanding is observing the phenomena outside of it, without bias or predisposition. Thus, Choice *E* is wrong.

26. B: The electrons passed through both holes and then onto the plate. Choices *A, C,* and *E* are wrong because such movement is not mentioned at all in the text. In the passage, the author says that electrons that were physically observed appeared to pass through one hole or another. Remember, the electrons that were observed doing this were described as acting like particles. Therefore, Choice D is wrong. Recall that the plate actually recorded electrons passing through both holes simultaneously and hitting the plate This behavior—the electron activity that wasn't seen by humans—was characteristic of waves. Thus, Choice *B* is the right answer.

27. C: The author uses "gravity" to demonstrate an example of natural phenomena humans discovered and understood without the use of tools or machines. Choice *A* mirrors the language in the beginning of the paragraph, but is incorrect in its intent. Choice *B* is incorrect; the paragraph mentions nothing of "not knowing the true nature of gravity." Choices *D* and *E* are both incorrect as well. There is no mention of an "alternative solution" or "looking forward" to new technology in this paragraph.

28. E: The important thing to keep in mind is that we must choose a scenario that best parallels, or is most similar to, the discovery of the experiment mentioned in the passage. The important aspects of the experiment can be summed up like so: humans directly observed one behavior of electrons and then through analyzing a tool (the plate that recorded electron hits), discovered that there was another electron behavior that could not be physically seen by human eyes. This best parallels the scenario in Choice *E*. Like Feynman, the colorblind person is able to observe one aspect of the world but through the special goggles (a tool) he is able to see a natural phenomenon that he could not physically see on his own. While Choice *D* is compelling because an x-ray helps humans see the broken bone, it is not necessarily revealing that the bone is broken in the first place. The other choices do not parallel the scenario in question. Therefore, Choice *E* is the best choice.

29. A, C: The first sentence of the second paragraph states, "While spending more than other countries per capita on health care services, the United States spends less on average than do other nations on social services impacting social and behavioral determinants of health." Thus, Choices *A* and *C* are the correct answers. Choice *B* is incorrect because it reverses the United States' ratio. The author argues that America's lower life expectancy is due to lower spending on social services, not insufficient funding for health care, so Choice *D* is incorrect. Choice *E* is incorrect because the United States does fund

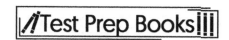

interdisciplinary programs that include behavioral and social science, like the Clinical and Translational Science Awards.

30. B: The Clinical and Translational Science Awards are mentioned in the third paragraph, and the author states that its interdisciplinary programs "aim to advance the translation of research findings from 'bench' to 'bedside' to 'community.'" Thus, Choice *B* is the correct answer. The Clinical and Translational Science Awards would likely support expanding social services, but advocating for that position isn't their purpose, so Choice *A* is incorrect. Similarly, the Clinical and Translational Science Awards likely conduct research on behavioral risks, but that's only part of the larger goal. So Choice *C* is incorrect. Choice *D* is incorrect because employing social and behavioral scientists is not the Clinical and Translational Science Awards' primary purpose. It's unclear whether the Clinical and Translational Science Awards would even be involved in policy questions like calculating the optimal ratio for government spending, so Choice *E* isn't the primary purpose.

31. C: The author repeatedly mentions how the United States neglects social services. According to the author, this is why the United States performs poorly on key health indicators despite spending more per capita on health care than any other country. In addition, the author argues that the Clinical and Translational Science Awards should hire more social and behavioral scientists. Thus, Choice *C* is the correct answer. Choices *A* and *D* are premises that support the conclusion, not the main thesis, so they are both incorrect. Choice *B* is incorrect because it's only providing background information about the Clinical and Translational Science Awards. The author never asserts that life expectancy is the most important health care indicator, and, even if that were true, it wouldn't be the main thesis. Thus, Choice *E* is incorrect.

32. C: In lines 6 and 7, it is stated that avarice can prevent a man from being necessitously poor, but too timorous, or fearful, to achieve real wealth. According to the passage, avarice does not tend to make a person very wealthy. The passage states that oppression, not avarice, is the consequence of wealth. The passage does not state that avarice drives a person's desire to be wealthy.

33. D: Paine believes that the distinction that is beyond a natural or religious reason is between king and subjects. He states that the distinction between good and bad is made in heaven. The distinction between male and female is natural. He does not mention anything about the distinction between humans and animals.

34. A: The passage states that the Heathens were the first to introduce government by kings into the world. The quiet lives of patriarchs came before the Heathens introduced this type of government. It was Christians, not Heathens, who paid divine honors to living kings. Heathens honored deceased kings. Equal rights of nature are mentioned in the paragraph, but not in relation to the Heathens.

35. B: Paine asserts that a monarchy is against the equal rights of nature and cites several parts of scripture that also denounce it. He doesn't say it is against the laws of nature. Because he uses scripture to further his argument, it is not despite scripture that he denounces the monarchy. Paine addresses the law by saying the courts also do not support a monarchical government.

36. A: To be *idolatrous* is to worship idols or heroes, in this case, kings. It is not defined as being deceitful. While idolatry is considered a sin, it is an example of a sin, not a synonym for it. Idolatry may have been considered illegal in some cultures, but it is not a definition for the term.

37. B: Mr. Button's wife is about to have a baby. The passage begins by giving the reader information about traditional birthing situations. Then, we are told that Mr. and Mrs. Button decide to go against tradition to have their baby in a hospital. The next few passages are dedicated to letting the reader know how Mr. Button dresses and goes to the hospital to welcome his new baby. There is a doctor in this excerpt, as Choice *C* indicates, and Mr. Button does put on clothes, as Choice *D* indicates. However, Mr. Button is not going to the doctor's office nor is he about to go shopping for new clothes.

38. A: The tone of the above passage is nervous and excited. We are told in the fourth paragraph that Mr. Button "arose nervously." We also see him running without caution to the doctor to find out about his wife and baby—this indicates his excitement. We also see him stuttering in a nervous yet excited fashion as he asks the doctor if it's a boy or girl. Though the doctor may seem a bit abrupt at the end, indicating a bit of anger or shame, neither of these choices is the overwhelming tone of the entire passage. Despite the circumstances, joy and gratitude are not the main tone in the passage.

39. D: To introduce the setting of the story and its characters. We know we are being introduced to the setting because we are given the year in the very first paragraph along with the season: "one day in the summer of 1860." This is a classic structure of an introduction of the setting. We are also getting a long explanation of Mr. Button, what his work is, who is related to him, and what his life is like in the third paragraph.

40. A: To explain the setting of the narrative and give information about the story. The setting of a narrative is the time and place. We see from the first paragraph that the year is 1860. We also can discern that it is summer, and Mr. and Mrs. Button are about to have a baby. This tells us both the setting and information about the story.

41. D: Something is unusual about the birth of the baby. The word "curious" is thrown in at the end twice, which tells us the doctor is suspicious about something having to do with the birth of the baby, since that is the most recent event to happen. Mr. Button is acting like a father who is expecting a baby, and the doctor seems confused about something.

Sentence Equivalence

42. B, E: *Barren* means deserted, void, lifeless, or having little. *Infertile* means unable to produce life, which mirrors barren. A desert is barren because it produces little vegetation. *Fruitful, sumptuous, feracious* and *lavish* express richness and abundance, which contradict *barren* and *infertile*.

43. C, D: From the Latin root *liber*, meaning free, *liberate* means to free or release. *Release* is synonymous with *liberate*. *Agitate* and *plague* both mean to annoy, which is not the same as the meaning in this sentence. *Instigate* can mean to start, which is not synonymous with liberate. *Fracture* is to crack or break something, which can metaphorically be attributed to liberation (breaking of chains), but is not directly related to the word liberate.

44. C, F: Jackson wanted to relieve his *parched* or *arid* throat. *Parched* and *arid* are the correct answers because they mean *dry* or *thirsty*. Choice *A*, humid, means moist, and usually refers to the weather. Choice *B*, scorched, means blackened or baked, and doesn't fit in this context. While Jackson's throat could have been dusty, Choice *D*, from playing baseball, one usually doesn't need to relieve a dusty throat, but instead clean it. Choice *E*, dissonant, is usually a term used in music to describe discordant harmony.

45. A, E: The two friends became more *attached* and *inseparable*. For this question, it's important to look at the context of the sentence. The second sentence says the friends shared good memories on the trip, which would not make the friends distant or irritable, Choices *B* and *D*. Choice *C* does not

grammatically fit within the sentence: "became more suffering" is incorrect usage. Therefore, Choices *A* and *E* are correct.

46. A, B: She *promised* or *guaranteed* her fans the sequel would be just as exciting as the first. Choice *C*, invigorated, means energized, and might fit the tone of the sentence with the word *excited*. However, *promised* is the better word to use here. Choice *D*, germinated, means to grow. Choice *E*, denied, is the opposite of the word *promised* and does not fit with the word *excited*. Choice *F*, *warned*, is incorrect because it doesn't fit in with the context; Kira wouldn't *warn* that the book would be exciting because those two words have conflicting tones.

47. C, E: My hands started *shaking* or *trembling* and my heart stopped. Usually when someone is afraid or nervous, their hands start to shake. *Tremble* is a synonym of *shake*. Choice *A*, dancing, does not make sense in the context of the sentence. Choice *B*, glowing, is incorrect; hands usually do not glow when one is afraid of something. Choice *D*, throbbing, is closer than *A* or *B*, but Choices *C* and *E*, shaking and trembling, are better answers than *throbbing*. Choice *F*, pulsating, is not the correct movement; this means more like *bouncing* or *jumping*.

48. B, D: To *belittle* or *disparage* someone is to put them down. Although this may involve breaking a spirit and causing despair, *despair* is the result of disparage. To *spar* or *fight* may also be a result of disparage. *Endorse* is incorrect because it means to approve. *Belittle* means to bring someone down with words and is synonymous with *disparage*.

49. A, C: The runners *sprinted* or *dashed* toward the finish line. Choice *B* is incorrect; runners who begin a race usually don't skip toward the finish line. Choice *D*, herded, means to gather around something; usually *herded* is used for animals and not for runners. Choice *E* does not fit within the context of the sentence, as normally runners would be *sprinting* and not *rejoicing* toward a finish line. Choice *F*, amassed, means to gather, so this is not the best answer choice. After the shot, the runners would be running or sprinting or dashing, not *gathering*.

50. B, F: *Chastise* and *rebuke* mean to reprimand severely. *Honor, choose,* and *locate* are unrelated. Both *rebuke* and *chastise* are verbs, making both a match. *Stagnate* means to stand still or fester, so this doesn't fit with the mother's situation here.

Dear GRE Test Taker,

We would like to start by thanking you for purchasing this study guide for your GRE exam. We hope that we exceeded your expectations.

Our goal in creating this study guide was to cover all of the topics that you will see on the verbal sections of the test. We also strove to make our practice questions as similar as possible to what you will encounter on test day. With that being said, if you found something that you feel was not up to your standards, please send us an email and let us know.

We would also like to let you know about other books in our catalog that may interest you.

Test Name	Amazon Link
MCAT	amazon.com/dp/1628458534
GMAT	amazon.com/dp/1628456981

We have study guides in a wide variety of fields. If the one you are looking for isn't listed above, then try searching for it on Amazon or send us an email.

Thanks Again and Happy Testing!
Product Development Team
info@studyguideteam.com

Interested in buying more than 10 copies of our product? Contact us about bulk discounts:
bulkorders@studyguideteam.com

FREE Test Taking Tips DVD Offer

To help us better serve you, we have developed a Test Taking Tips DVD that we would like to give you for FREE. **This DVD covers world-class test taking tips that you can use to be even more successful when you are taking your test.**

All that we ask is that you email us your feedback about your study guide. Please let us know what you thought about it – whether that is good, bad or indifferent.

To get your **FREE Test Taking Tips DVD**, email freedvd@studyguideteam.com with "FREE DVD" in the subject line and the following information in the body of the email:

     a. The title of your study guide.

     b. Your product rating on a scale of 1-5, with 5 being the highest rating.

     c. Your feedback about the study guide. What did you think of it?

     d. Your full name and shipping address to send your free DVD.

If you have any questions or concerns, please don't hesitate to contact us at freedvd@studyguideteam.com.

Thanks again!

Made in the USA
Middletown, DE
02 October 2021